NEW YORK STATE ENGLISH COUNCIL MONOGRAPHS

SERIES EDITOR:

James L. Collins

State University of New York at Buffalo

EDITORIAL COMMITTEE

James Collins

William McCleary

Carol Jamieson

NEW YORK STATE ENGLISH COUNCIL

John A. Andola, Executive Secretary

Liverpool Central Schools

Wetzel Road

Liverpool, N.Y. 13088

THE NEW YORK STATE ENGLISH COUNCIL

AN ASSOCIATION OF TEACHERS OF ENGLISH LANGUAGE AND LITERATURE

ISBN: 0-930348-09-5

TABLE OF CONTENTS

Introduction ... i

I. PROCESS

The Composing Process: A New Model for Teaching Composition ... 1
    Ann O. Gebhard

The Reading-Writing Connection ... 10
    Charlotte Klose

Written Composition in Early Childhood: A Developmental Process ... 21
    Adelle Jacobs

Building a Fictional World: Motivating Writing Through Variety ... 28
    Terence D. Mosher

The Composing Process and Its Relationship to the Teaching of Writing ... 46
    Robert W. Blake

Teaching Writing Skills Through Peer Evaluation ... 65
    Jerome F. Megna

II. PRODUCT

The Young Student Writers ... 79
    Charles R. Chew

Students Compose: Writer's Workshop ... 91
    Sheila A. Schlawin and Charles R. Chew

Speculations About Student Writing As Seen On Statewide Tests ... 101
    Sheila A. Schlawin

III. PROGRAM

The Program for Effective Writing: How to Establish it, How to Control it ... 109
    Kenneth Kahn

Designing a K-12 Writing Program One District's Response to the Two Revolutions in English ... 133
    John Andola

In-Service: A Cure for Sick Writing Programs ... 151
    Doris Quick

Introduction

Process, Product, Program. In exploring these three major areas of written composition, the essays in this monograph repeatedly bring to mind a fourth, equally alliterative, concern: Practice.

The adage "Practice makes perfect" carries a double meaning for composition, and this monograph treats both meanings. First, there is writing practice. No one learns to write without actually writing. Then there are teaching practices. Sound and careful instructions are necessary for students to develop writing abilties. The strength of this monograph lies in its discussion of these two types of practice.

In the six essays in the *Process* section, the focus is on writing practice, on the types of activities that build composition skills. In the six essays in the *Product* and *Program* sections, the focus shifts to professional practice, to the types of activities that teach writing and that build writing programs. The monograph is intended for an audience of teachers and administrators, and its subject is writing and the teaching of writing. Its purpose is to influence practice. Throughout the monograph the emphasis keeps coming back to what student writers and their teachers ought to be doing.

That emphasis is needed because we know too little about successful practice in the composition classroom. Research and theory are often too esoteric and jargon-laden to be useful to teachers. Similarly, methods textbooks are often too glib and superficial to have any meaningful impact on classroom realities. Important practical questions have slipped unanswered between research and teaching. What do studies of the writing process imply for writing practice? How to provide real audiences for student writers in crowded classrooms? How to use models of good writing and rhetorical devices? What is the appropriate role for the composition textbook or handbook? And what about spelling, mechanics, vocabulary, sentence combining, assignment-making?

These questions, and others, are on our minds as we teach writing, but we have little or no time to answer them. Consequently, we tend to trust to ourselves and our own designs. We close classroom doors and go about the business of teaching. How to examine the value of our efforts? How to look for connections across grade and ability levels, across classrooms, and across academic disciplines?

No book can answer all the practial questions about writing and the teaching of writing. This one, though, gets us moving in the right directions. It explores current knowledge of writing processes and identifies implications for writing practice. It finds patterns in written products and tells us what these patterns mean for teaching. It describes writing programs and how they develop. The rest, quite appropriately, is up to us, to teachers and administrators responsible for finally implementing answers to key practical questions.

The first essay in the *Process* section surveys theories of the composing process and shows how theory can be applied in the classroom. Here Gebhard provides help with setting goals, sequencing assignments, and selecting activities for pre-writing, composing, and post-writing. In the second essay, Klose explores parallels and connections between reading and writing. She advocates a learning by doing stance for both teachers and students, and she discusses the diagnosis of skills and problems in each of the two halves of literacy. Klose takes a developmental view of the writing process, a view which is expanded in the next essay in which Jacobs examines writing in the early childhood years. Here we are introduced to the concept of writing readiness and to important relationships between writing and other composing behaviors, such as drawing and dictating.

These first three essays offer a good deal of advice on writing practice and teaching practices, and this advice is exemplified and made concrete in the next three essays. Mosher takes us inside a high school classroom and describes a successful unit which incorporates many types of writing for diverse audiences and purposes. The unit is comprehensive, varied, and meaningful; what's more, it is fun. In the next essay, Blake describes the complexities involved in a full understanding of the writing process. More importantly, he tells how to manage these complexities by giving us detailed lists of activities for each stage in the process. Both Mosher and Blake include peer audiences in their designs for the teaching and writing, and that subject is treated fully in the last essay of the *Process* section where Megna describes a peer group methods of evaluating student writing.

The three essays in the *Product* section of this monograph examine writers and teachers at work, and they also take a close look at the results of that labor. In the Chew essay, we are taken inside a first grade classroom where students are below average, but their writing is not. Chew describes them as prolific, confident writers, and he identifies the activities that make them that way. Using essays from students in grades 2 through 5, Chew goes on to clarify and illustrate the many skills apparent in children's writing. The message is that children can write, and that message is extended in the next essay where Chew and Schlawin describe a successful writing workshop for fourth, fifth, sixth graders. Here the authors discuss the knowledge and assumptions they brought to their teaching, their teaching activities, and the results--enthusiastic writers and improved writing. In the final essay in this section, Schlawin identifies characteristics of compositions written for the Regents Competency Test in Writing. From these written products she carefully reasons to implications for classroom practices.

The *Program* section of this monograph deals with planning and implementing writing programs that cut across the usual boundaries: grades, abilities, classrooms, teachers, even schools. In the first essay, Kahn identifies important elements of program management. He shows how these elements are related and how they can be organized and controlled by administrators. The next essay describes one school district's experience with the task of developing a new writing program. Here Andola provides a detailed analysis of the content, scope, and evolution of his district's writing program, and he offers several recommendations for other districts facing the same task. Throughout the essay, Andola places confidence in the ability of teachers to develop and implement writing programs, and that theme continues in the final essay where Quick argues for in-service opportunities to strengthen writing programs. She concludes with a list of guidelines which emphasize teacher abilities to improve writing practice and teaching practices.

The essays in this monograph provide a broad analysis of written composition. The analysis, though, is focused: on process, product, and program, and on practice. The message, finally, is not only that practice makes perfect. The message is also that practice can be perfected.

James L. Collins
Monographs Editor
New York State English Council

I. PROCESS

THE COMPOSING PROCESS: A NEW MODEL FOR TEACHING COMPOSITION

Ann O. Gebhard

Ithaca College

In the 1963 *Research in Written Composition*, authors Braddock, Lloyd-Jones and Schoer write that "little has been proved about the instructional factors influencing composition." Seventeen years of effort have not substantially changed the truth of that statement. What has changed is the focus of attention for investigator and instructor alike from the product of composition to its process. Composition teachers today are the beneficiaries of this change, a healthy if quiet revolution, brought about by the congruence of a number of developments both within and without the profession.

During the 1960's an unprecedented number of young people completed high school and sought higher education. Questioning and unorthodox, these students tended to emphasize private rather than public meaning. Perceptive teachers responded by making greater provision in composition programs for personal writing. Condemning the pompous and artificial prose sometimes encouraged by traditional programs, which he called "Engfish," Ken Macrorie (1968) called anew for instruction emphasizing direct observation and the expression of personal thoughts and feelings. (Progressives like Hughes Mearns in *Creative Power* (1929) and Wilbur Hatfied in the National Council's *Experience Curriculum for English* (1935) had made this point decades before.) In *Word, Self and Reality: The Rhetoric*, James E. Miller reflected a similar position; young writers were advised:

> The language that never leaves our head is like colorful yarn, endlessly spun out multicolored threads dropping into a void, momentarily compacted, entangled, fascinating, elusive. . .
> Writing that is discovery forces the capturing, the retrieving, the bringing into focus these stray

and random thoughts. Sifting through them we make decisions that are as much about the self as about langauge. Indeed, writing is largely a proces of choosing among alternatives from images and thoughts of the endless flow, and this choosing... becomes in effect the making up one's self.

Such analysis not only reflected the social context of the period but also a developing body of knowledge about language derived from the sciences of psychology and linguistics. Structural linguistics had established the important concept of the primacy of oral language; now generative-transformational linguistics was attempting to trace the complex relationship of thought and utterance.

Theoretical advances had important and seemingly contradictory consequences in the evolution of the composing process. From structural linguistics had long since come the proposition that written English be considered a distinct dialect with its own conventions, obviously different from those of spoken language, to secure meaning. Researchers O'Donnell, Griffen, and Norris (1967) found evidence that in grade five and seven students, control of syntax was further advanced in writing than in speech. Vygotsky, the Russian psychologist, declared that the two modes may reflect distinct thought processes (1962).

> Written speech is a separate linguistic function, differing from oral speech in both structure and mode of functioning. Even its minimal development requires a high level of abstraction.

At the same time "speech act" theorists were advising teachers to root their instruction firmly within a communicative context. This meant permitting verbalization to serve as a solid base for writing. In "Talk-Write: A Behavioral Pedagogy for Composition" (1969) Zoellner condemned "the pervasively defining instrumental metaphor in our teaching of composition ... that written word is thought on paper" and advocated adapting principles of operant conditioning to help youngsters shape oral into written utterance. Tovatt and Miller (1967) advised teachers to adapt an Oral-Aural-Visual strategy in which students speak into a tape recorder while composing and simultaneously hear the tapes played back while reading the written transcripts. Their work specifically links the psycholinguistic processes of speech and writing:

> It may be postulated that speech strategies or oral strategies which the individual develops and modifies at one level of abstraction could form the neural bases for developing a refining writing strategies (that) he forms at a higher level of abstraction.

Few developments during this period were more important in focussing attention on process than the revival of professional interest in rhetoric, confirmed in 1965 by the publication of E.P.J. Corbett's influential *Classical Rhetoric for the Modern Student*. Emphasizing pre-writing invention, the new rhetorics advanced a problem-solving approach to writing instruction and stressed the essential triadic relationship of form, purpose, and audience. The new rhetoric reminded teachers of the existence of other modes of discourse (narration, description, and persuasion) as well as the typically assigned exposition. Traditionally, school-writing past the elementary grades had tended to be relentlessly expository and had represented the antirhetorical situation in which the writer composed for a reader, thoroughly knowledgable about the subject, whose sole purpose in reading was evaluation. Both communication theory and rhetoric stressed the importance of meaningful writing tasks directed to real audiences.

Also during this period there began to emerge a developmental model for teaching composition. In *Teaching the Universe of Discourse* (1968) James Moffett charts the "spectrum of discourse" in terms of a hierarchy of levels of abstraction that ranges from the act of "recording, the drama of what is happening" to "reporting, the narrative of what happened," through "generalizing, the exposition of what happens," to the most abstact level, "theorizing, the argumentation of what will, may happen."

The British educator/researcher James Britton provides another, but theoretically consonant, developmental model. For Britton, like Moffett, "talk is the sea on which all else floats." The inheritor of a philosophic-linguistic tradition which espouses the subjective nature of reality, Britton sees language as shaping as well as expressing the child's perception of experience. Britton (1977) and his fellow researchers of the British School Study Council urge that the young writer initially be encouraged to compose expressively, to write subjective, personal response to experience. This research indicates that too early efforts to have the writer package such experience in tight little paragraphs, perhaps headed by a topic sentence, may cause the child to distort the nature of the experience to satisfy the requirements of the assignment. (In David Holbrook's term "to tell neat little lies.") Britton speculates that "expressive writing may operate as a matrix from which differentiated forms of mature writing are developed." He distinguishes expressive writing from "transactional," reader-directed informative or persuasive writing, and also from form-conscious, imaginative writing, which he calls "poetic." Both developmental models stress the interactive nature of growth in language skill: one element of such interaction involves the perceptive of experience, emphasizing the covert processes through which young pupils construct and organize their unique realities; another element stresses the overt interaction of the child with his peers, teachers, family, through which perceptions are realized and expressed in social language.

Obviously, a major change in instruction so basic to the curriculum as writing occurs over time as a result of new attitudes, knowledge, and techniques. This summary has attempted to outline but a few of the contributions of the last two decades that have resulted in theories of the composing process. Essentially, it is the matter of application of theory that interests the classroom teacher. What do these developments in the composing process mean when theory is translated into action in the classroom?

The first step is applying theory in the establishment of goals. Traditional instruction has set control of written form as a primary goal; focus was on the student's ability to produce a coherent, error-free expository essay. To implement the composing process, teachers need to reconceptualize this goal, not by putting it completely aside, but by considering carefully the means to this end. Just as in the youngster's first-language acquisition, fluency in written language precedes control.

Thus, within the model of the composing process, the teacher's first goal becomes to encourage in students the confidence in writing that promotes fluency. The classroom atmosphere should be supportive, a place where individuals feel they can take risks and where classmates are encouraged to share and help one another. In *Strategies for Teaching the Composing Process* (1978) Koch and Brazil, call this "the comfort zone." The manual of the successful New York City writing program WEDGE contains a questionnaire "Model Writing Classroom" which asserts, "A climate of trust is created so that students trust both classmates and teachers to deal with writing sensitively."

Inherent in such a classroom climate is the teacher's ability to sequence writing tasks so that in composition as in other school subjects, instruction moves from the simple to the complex, from the concrete to the abstract. Teachers need to encourage youngsters to write in a variety of modes, perhaps beginning with personal narrative and description, methods of development rooted in the student's direct experience of time and space relationships. In a study conducted at the University of Arkansas, Karen Hodge (1980) based an experimental course on developmental stages, sequencing her class assignments roughly in the order recommended by Moffett. When pre and post tests of the experimental group were compared at the end of the semester with those of a control group, results showed the "91% of the experimental group improved in theoretical writing -- the highest range of the developmental ladder -- compared to 59% of the control group whose assignments were in random rather than sequential order."

In choosing assignments the teacher must also consider the rhetorical situation, the purpose and audience of a particular task, and help students in this understanding. What is the purpose of writing? For whom is the writing intended? The stipulation of these elements within assignments and their clarification in terms of the writer's task in the classroom is essential.

Teachers need to make provision for self-selection of writing topics. Janet Emig's research found that gifted secondary students were motivated by the opportunity to write "reflectively" on topics important to them.

How then is this process implemented? The three stages of the composing process are pre-writing, the activities manifest or hidden that precede actual writing itself, the act of composing, getting the words written down, along with the preliminary editing that occurs as one writes, and post-writing, everything that happens after the first draft is written, including revision and publication.

Inspired by communication and psycholinguistic theory, pre-writing activities stress the relationship of writing to speech and thought. As stated earlier, writing isn't merely talk written down, but, for many students, discussion furnishes an absolutely essential base because it generates both ideas and language that can be put to use. Talk can occur in teacher-led or small-group discussion or through role-play; Terry Radcliffe (1972) recommends pupil-pairing, a questioning procedure, and recording of the resulting dialogue as a preparation for writing.

Pre-writing activities may also include the use of models and the direct teaching of a specific writing-related skill. It may also involve a discussion of the criteria by which the writing will be evaluated. The students may create their own check-list of items which are important to the assignment, one that can be used later in revision.

Pre-writing instruction may include the use of specific discovery procedures. Odell (1974) studied the effect of one procedure and found evidence that the operations advocated were at least partly reflected in student performance. In *Writing as a Process of Discovery,* Jenkinson and Seybold suggest questioning procedures for helping students discover what they know or do not know about the subject. The development of questions to be researched can be an important part of the brainstorming and discussion that precedes transactional writing. Such prewriting sessions may also look toward the final form that the writing will take as the teacher helps students to see logical relationships within their subject and to choose appropriate methods or organizaton.

In sum, pre-writing may consist of a number of enabling activities. A study by Graves (1973) of seven-year olds concludes "that many variables contribute in unique ways at any given point in the process of writing." Graves found that drawing and the presence of concrete objects can be important to composing at this level. In this study, also, students' self-selection of topics encouraged writing fluency.

The writing part of the process should be done in class with the teacher acting as helpful editor, Writing success teaches a lot more than failure. Petty (1978) reports of two studies of children's writing processes which examine student and class procedures. Sawkins (1978) concluded that "children probably would seek more help if they thought it would be given" and Stallard (1974) found that time factors are extremely important to the encouragement of good writing.

After the student has completed his or her first draft, the post-writing phase emphasizes the importance of the writing as communication. The key question becomes "Does this writing say to the reader what was intended?" The writer finds out by sharing the work with peers, a most significant audience for young people. The first sharing should probably be read aloud by the writers to help them retain a measure of control; typically students self-correct as they read.

In terms of process, revision is important in post-writing. There is a sense in which it is true that no student's paper is poor, just inadequately revised. Generally, students keep their work in writing folders. All assignments are completed to the point where they can be shared, but not all assignments are extensively revised for summative evaluation and publication. Throughout the composing process there is acknowledgement of actual practice. Even professional writers make false starts; not every scrap of writing undergoes extensive revision so that it can eventually merit publication; much may be discarded along the way. The writing folder permits students to make comparable decisions. Perhaps with teacher guidance, the student selects from among the first or second drafts in the folder the ones that merit revision and submission. At this point in the process the writer has had help from the teacher in editing and from his classmates in directions for improvement. In *Writing Without Teachers,* Peter Elbow describes one successful writing workshop approach in which the writer's classmates provide such direction. More help can now be forthcoming.

To complete the process, the finished composition is published. This can be on the classroom bulletin board or library table, or it can be more ambitious. Eliot Wigginton's successful *Foxfire* magazine testifies to the power of creatively managed student prose. In some schools youngsters are involved in helping edit and write trade magazines, local government bulletins, or their own publishing ventures.

Thus the composing process calls for attention to purpose and audience, for inclusion of pre-writing activites, for provision of time to write in class, for feedback and revision in a supportive atmosphere, and, finally, for acknowledgement of student efforts through publication.

Rooted firmly in contemporary rhetorical and psycholinguistic theory, this model for composition instruction also makes good common sense. It provides a method for teachers to support students through the process of personal and intellectual growth that writing especially affords and enhances.

Bibliography

Braddock, Richard, Lloyd-Jones, Richard, & Schoer, Lowell. *Research in Written Composition.* Champaign, Illinois: National Council of Teachers of English, 1963.

Britton, J. L., Burgess, T., Martin, N., McLeod. A., & Rosen, H. *The Development of Writing Abilities.* London: MacMillan Education, 1975.

Corbett, E. P. J. *Classical Rhetoric for the Modern Student.* New York: Oxford University Press. 1965.

Emig, Janet. *The Composing Processes of Twelfth Graders* (NCTE Research Report No. 13). Urbana, Illinois: National Council of Teachers of English, 1971.

Graves, Donald. "An Examination of the Writing Processes of Seven-Year Old Children." *Research in the Teaching of English*, 1975, *9*, 227-241.

Hodges, Karen. *Proposed Stages of Writing Development: A Curriculum for Composition.* Unpublished paper. University of Arkansas, 1980.

Jenkinson, Edward B., & Seybold, Donald A. *Writing as a Process of Discovery.* Bloomington, Indiana: Indiana University Press. 1970.

Koch, Carl, and Brazil, James M. *Strategies for Teaching the Composition Process.* Urbana, Illinois: National Council of Teachers of English, 1978.

Macrorie, Ken. *Uptaught.* New York: Hayden Book Company, 1968.

Mearns, Hughes. *Creative Power: The Education of Youth in the Creative Arts.* Chicago: University of Chicago, 1929.

Moffett, James. *Teaching the Universe of Discourse.* New York: Houghton Mifflin Company, 1968.

National Council of Teachers of English. *An Experience Curriculum in English: Report of the Curriculum Commission,* Wilbur Hatfield, Chairman. New York: D. Appleton Century Company, Inc., 1935.

Odell, Lee. "Measuring the Effect of Instruction in Pre-Writing." *Research in the Teaching of English,* 1974, *8*, 223-240.

O'Donnell, Roy C., Griffin, William J., & Norris, Raymond C. "The Syntax of Kindergarten and Elementary Children." Champaign, Urbana: National Council of Teachers of Englsh, 1967.

Petty, Walter T. "The Writing of Young Children." In Charles Cooper and Lee Odell (Eds.), *Research on Composing: Points of Departure.* Urbana, Illinois: National Council of Teachers of English, 1978.

Radcliffe, Terry. "Talk-Write Composition: A Theoretical Model Proposing the Use of Speech to Improve Writing." *Research in the Teaching of English, 6,* 1972, 187-191.

Tovatt, Anthony & Miller, Ebert L. "The Sound of Writing." *Research in the Teaching of English, 1.* 1967.

Wedge - A Manual for the Secondary School English Class. New York: Division of Educational Planning and Support, Board of Education of the City of New York, 1978.

Zoellner, Robert. "Talk-Write: A Behavioral Pedagogy for Composition." *College English, 30,* 1969, 267-320.

THE READING-WRITING CONNECTION
Charlotte Klose

"Reading maketh a full man; conference a ready man; and writing an exact man." Francis Bacon thus perceived a relationship between reading and writing back in the seventeenth century. Now, concerned about the recent parallel decline in students' reading and writing skills, others, both in and out of the classroom, are seeing new connections between these two strands. Kenneth Goodman has compared the two. He describes reading as a receptive language process in which meaning is decoded and users get meaning from written language, and writing as a productive language process in which language is encoded and users go from language to meaning.[1] Reading and writing are the two sides of a single coin.

Current research into the biochemistry of the central nervous system strongly suggests that the neurological makeup of the individual plays a key role in the development of both reading and writing abilities. It is well documented that auditory or visual imperception can cause a host of reading difficulties. According to Janet Emig, "There may be biological bases for composing behaviors."[2] It seems that certain writing problems also may be neurologically based. One of the perceptual skills required for effective reading is figure-ground discrimination. This skill allows the child to recognize a given object in relation to its background. Impaired figure-ground perception results in an inability to focus attention upon relevant aspects of the visual field while tuning out extraneous background stimuli.[3] A child with this deficit seems inattentive and disorganized because his/her attention tends to jump to any intruding stimulus; he/she cannot pick out the relevant details on a page or a picture. How does this perceptual skill relate to writing ability? Janet Emig explains:

> Writing seems to require the establishment of firm figure-ground relations -- of what shall be stressed, perhaps through the deployment of superordinates, and what shall be subordinated, through the literal deployment of subordinate phrases and clauses. Persons with

organic, chemical, or psychological impairments . . . often cannot distinguish between elements that are incorporating and those that are illustrative."[4]

Other sensory and perceptual skills seem to be as essential to writing as to reading. For instance, Mina Shaughnessy listed these as requisite skills for re-scanning and re-working one's sentences: "a memory for unheard sentences, an ability to store verbal patterns visually from left to right, as in reading, and, beyond this, an ability to suspend closure of those patterns until, through additions, deletions, substitutions, or arrangements, the words fit the intended meaning."[5]

There are less theoretical connections between reading and writing as well. A list of "Some Obvious Truths about Writing" includes these observations:

> It is an internal process; its internal process is only accessible through consciousness of oneself; it is hierarchical in time; it is overwhelmingly "synthetic" rather than "analytic"; it requires a training of one's ears and voice; it is a system of arbitrary signs; it is dependent on speech.[6]

Is not each of these statements equally descriptive of reading? Included in a list of "Principles of Teaching Reading" are these:

> Learning to read is a complicated process; reading is a language process; learning to read is an individual process; reading instruction should be an organized, systematic, growth-producing activity; each child's weaknesses and needs must be diagnosed; the diagnosis must be used as a blueprint for instruction; learning to read is a long-term developmental process.[7]

Which of these principles is not directly applicable to writing instruction as well?

From research to pedagogy, the reading-writing connection is clear.

Understanding the process is the key to teaching both reading and writing. The teacher who knows the process of reading and the process of writing can teach both more effectively. Because teachers, like students, learn best by doing and not just by analyzing something, they need to read widely and themselves write to become very conscious of the processes involved and to internalize them. "Some books are to be tasted, others to be swallowed, and some few to be chewed and digested," also wrote Francis Bacon. Teachers who read with enough insight to perceive the truth of Bacon's analogy *are* qualified to teach students how to read selectively, how to read for a purpose, how to gauge rate, and how to judge credibility of sources. An Emily Dickinson poem begins, "There is no Frigate like a Book/To take us Lands away/ Nor any Coursers like a Page/Of prancing Poetry." Teachers who have themselves discovered the joy of reading and savor Dickinson's world of metaphor *are* equipped to teach students the power and the pleasure of words in print. Writing teachers, too, ought to be experiencing the process which they are trying to teach. Like a swimming coach who never gets into the water, such a writing teacher who does not practice writing has no direct experience with the process which he or she attempts to teach others. Lacking first-hand experience in composing, such teachers "underconceptualize and oversimplify the process of composing. Planning degenerates into outlining; reformulating becomes the correction of minor infelicities."[8] Even writing teachers who do write well cannot confidently rely on their own hazy memories of how they first learned to write. Rather, "the basis for deliberate teaching of others is learning how to observe what one does within oneself *here* and *now* to sustain one's facility in writing."[9] Such self-reflection is, of course, not easy, but it is absolutely essential. Expert knowledge of books about "how to read or write" simply cannot substitute for first-hand experience of what it means to function as a competent reader or writer. One who can analyze a sonata or a baseball play is not automatically equipped to perform in Carnegie Hall or to score a home run. No less is true of reading and writing.

Not only must teachers be experiencing the process which they purport to teach, they must allow students to experience it also. Teachers must make reading and writing conscious processes for students. This is not likely to happen if a teacher gives assignments for students to do in isolation and then grades them without followup. Such an approach is like that of a swimming coach who explains to a non-swimmer how to do the proper kick for the backstroke, orders practice on the gym floor without going near the water, and then warns that soon the non-swimmer will be expected to swim in a backstroke competition to be judged for the squad. Nor do students attain reading and writing skills by merely listening to lectures, taking notes, practicing isolated exercises, or reading about how to read or write. Certainly the swimming coach would not expect to see much improvement in the recruit simply because he or she had read the biography of a great backstroke swimmer. But if the novice swimmer studies films of that backstroke expert in action to learn techniques, then puts those techniques into practice while the coach observed this fledgeling performance and provided helpful feedback, considerable improvement might be expected. So it is with the teaching of reading and writing skills. These skills must be specifically taught, modelled, and practiced in ways meaningful to students.[10]

There seem to be natural stages in the child's acquisition of both reading and writing skills just as there are natural stages in the child's acquisition of listening and speaking skills. Various research studies support this hypothesis in reading.[11] And similarly, Janet Emig has described an apparent developmental sequence for students when they learn to write:

> Donald Grave thinks he can identify some markers of developing maturity in children from six to nine or ten.... There seems to be a longer, more elaborated process of writing for more sophisticated writers. There's also a contemplation of product. It seems that only skilled writers voluntarily do much rewriting or find pleasure in their own work. The student who is unhappy simply crumples the paper up and throws it away -- certain of the stages are omitted such as aesthetic pleasure when one is done.[12]

If learning to write is like learning to read a natural, sequential process, writing instruction ought to be developmentally structured. Yet most writing programs remain "predicated on the belief that there are established and widely accepted indices of written decorum and that student writers of all ages can learn and apply them."[13] Can student writers really learn and use given writing skills at any age? Can a first grader write a persuasive essay or a third grader a dramatic monologue? It seems unlikely. Jean Piaget's cognitive developmental psychology and James Moffett's theory of discourse lend considerable credence to the view that acquisition of writing skills may indeed be developmental in nature. If so, then careful sequencing of writing approaches and assignments becomes as vital in writing as well in reading instruction. Both reading and writing development are cyclical, not linear processes. A spiral movement, upward and outward, developing ever more sophisticated skills while broadening and strengthening the already acquired skills, informs a sound reading or writing program.

It is crucial to remember the individualness of learning to read and learning to write. John Berryman described the solitary nature of the writing process: "Writing is just a man alone in the room with the English language, trying to make it come out right." Just as each person's own neurological system, set of experiences, and combination of aptitudes and interests are unique to that individual, so is the mode of learning either to read or write. Ideally, the diagnosis and prescription of both reading and writing skills ought to be as carefully tailored to the individual as a doctor's medical care. The more a teacher knows of other processes and can simulate in his or her own mind each student's predicament and then develop an approach which will be challenging while ensuring success for that student, the more the teacher can genuinely be of help. To build solid reading and writing skills, it is imperative that the teacher possess the expertise and sensitivity to handle each student as a respected individual. Research has shown that students do not necessarily learn to read or write the way teachers think they do. Every teacher should be open to receive and consider new theories and explanations, modify the instructional approach accordingly, weigh the results, and then try something else when a tested method does not work.

As in reading, there is in writing no group problem

peculiar to third, sixth, ninth, or twelfth graders. The rigidity of the military inspection line is not transferable to the writing classroom. Students must be taught as individuals, not herded together by age, grade, height, or sex. All students, as they face a problem in their own writing, need a teacher who is prepared to help solve that particular problem. The order in which one individual encounters problems in writing -- and sometimes the problems themselves -- will not correspond to that of other students. And the time needed to solve these problems will vary.[14] It does not help to tell students *that* they are writing badly; the teacher must show the students *why* they are writing badly. The teacher needs to be flexible enough to provide a solution that will attack the root of each problem.

If students are told that twenty or thirty things are wrong with their papers, they, like the teacher, will be overwhelmed. But the teacher who has become an expert diagnostician can reduce most of these difficulties to a few central concerns, then zero in on and remedy the the most serious one first. A lack of structural unity, for instance, is far more serious than a few pronoun errors. By thus establishing priority, the teacher gains control over the writing program. In evaluating the next papers, the teacher can quickly see whether the one central problem is being solved. If so, another problem can be identified and attacked; if not, a new or repeated treatment can be prescribed. Using this "one problem at a time" approach will allow a teacher to help many more students with far less effort and with much more effectiveness. The typically overwhelming class load can be somewhat eased if the writing teacher does not try to treat all symptoms as equally serious but instead uses diagnostic expertise to identify and treat the key problems of each student. This ability is undoubtedly the writing teacher's most important asset. The ultimate test of skill in diagnosing comes when the teacher has trained students to diagnose their own problems. Before venturing an opinion, the teacher should ask students to give their own versions of what their individual writing problems are --the students may know them far better than the teacher can.[15] Certainly, teaching students how to identify and correct weaknesses in their own writing before submitting it reduces the teacher's paperload, but even more importantly, it makes the students independent writers and editors who are conscious of the writing process itself.[16] Developing this self-awareness and self-reliance in each writer is the central goal of a sound writing program. Most importantly, this entire approach, or any part of it, is equally applicable to a sound reading program.

No reading or writing teacher should try to prevent the learner from making errors. "Errors are valuable; they are the essential learning instrument.... Avoiding error is an inferior learning strategy to capitalizing on error."[17] There may be, in fact, a significant connection between the nature of reading and writing errors. It has been hypothesized that "systematic error in writing is correlated with reading disfunction,"[18] and various studies of good and poor readers reveal that reading errors made by poor readers correlate with writing errors made by developing writers.[19] Psycholinguistic theories stress the importance, even the necessity of "productive guesses" in learning to read. For the reader, a changing pattern of errors gradually emerges: "an increase in proficiency causes different, more sophisticated kinds of errors, errors which reflect an increased ability to glean the meaning of the text."[20] There is yet another value in studying patterns of reading errors. Numerous studies, especially those of Kenneth and Yetta Goodman, and including several described by R. M. Golinkoff, have revealed important kinds of silent and oral reading stretegies which readers use to process the written word.[21] Studying errors in writing can be equaly productive. "The fact that a writer makes an error is less signficant than how he or she came to make that error.... Errors are clues to the system of organized rules and intelligent strategies that a student draws on to perform a composing task."[22] Mistakes are positive evidence that a child is trying to express an increasing number of ideas and/or is attempting to combine these in ever more complex ways. A beginning writer who at first produced papers consisting of only a few short, "correct" sentences may suddenly write more sentences, but with errors -- if the teacher does not squelch these new efforts by insisting on absolute grammatical correctness. It is inevitable that as students attempt to create sentences which are more complex semantically and/or syntactically, they will make errors. The teacher ought to realize that many of these errors are recognizable, predictable, and natural to the learning process.[23] It is clear that student writers often make errors which signify progress rather than regression. Janet Emig describes teachers who fail to utilize student errors advantageously as "neurotic"; she sees little evidence that "the persistent pointing out of errors in student themes leads to the elimination of these errors, yet teachers spend much of their energy in this futile and unrewarding exercise."[24] This frenetic "red-pencil" approach is likely to intensify the neuroses of both teacher and students. On the other hand, the teacher who has learned to spot patterns of errors and use them productively in order to remedy students' reading and writing deficiencies is likely to see both solid improvement in those skills and happier students.

"I love to lose myself in other men's minds.... Books think for me," said Charles Lamb. "Writing and rewriting are a constant search for what one is saying," wrote John Updike. A century apart these two readers and writers have recognized the necessity of total involvement and careful thought in mastering the reading or the writing process. Both processes are active. Both can be learned. But the perfection of neither facility is sudden and effortless or mystical and intuitive. "The more a man writes, the more he can write," observed William Hazlitt; he could have acknowledged the same truth about reading.

Reading and writing can be taught if students are given the opportunity to discover for themselves and then to master the cumulative skills underlying each process. There are not only commonalties between reading and writing but also commonalities in the ways that students acquire the use of these vital language processes. No skills and abilities grow in isolation from content, and this interdependence is above all true of reading and writing. Determining the essentials of reading and writing instruction is a continuing process, far more demanding and significant than merely listing isolated skills assumed to be basic. Instruction in both skill areas must grow out of the content areas and be fused with them, or it is superfluous and useless. The interlocking aspects of language are being delineated by careful research, and the reading-writing connection is both intricate and significant. Its most important implication for teachers is that competent, interrelated instruction throughout the stages of each process, followed by guided, meaningful practice, does lead to competence in both strands. "The bookful blockhead, ignorantly read,/with loads of learned lumber in his head." Alexander Pope's satiric couplets depicts the student whose teacher has not seen and conveyed the reading and writing proceses. The antithesis of this image, one who can read and write to the best of his or her potential, is the goal for every student and for every teacher.

[1] Kenneth S. Goodman, "Linguistically Sound Research in Reading," in *Improving Reading Research*, eds. Roger Far et al. (Newark, Delaware, 1976), p. 89.

[2] Janet Emig, *The Composing Processes of Twelfth Graders* (Urbana, Ill., 1971), p. 69.

[3] Robert Farrald and Richard Schamber, *A Diagnostic and Prescriptive Technique* (Sioux Falls, S.D., 1973), p. 238.

[4] Emig, p. 69.

[5] Mina P. Shaughnesy, *Errors and Expectations* (New York, 1977), p. 80.

[6] Bill Bernhardt, *Just Writing* (New York, 1977), pp. 14-16.

[7] Arthur W. Heilman, *Principles and Practices of Teaching Reading* (Columbus, Ohio, 1972), pp. 4-11.

[8] Emig, p. 98.

[9] Bernhardt, p. 13.

[10] Leon Williams, "Toward a Realistic Teacher Workload," *English Journal*, LXVIV (May 1980), p. 9.

[11] Constance Weaver, *Grammar for Teachers* (Urbana, Ill., 1979), p. 11.

[12] Lois Rose, "An Interview with Janet Emig," *English Journal*, LXVIII (October 1979), pp. 12-13.

[13] Emig, p. 38.

[14] Donald M. Murray, *A Writer Teaches Writing* (Boston, 1968), p. 106.

[15] Murray, p. 130.

[16] Gene Stanford, ed., *How to Handle the Paper Load* (Urbana, Ill., 1979), p. xiv.

[17] James Moffett, *Teaching the Universe of Discourse* (Boston, 1968), p. 199.

[18] Patrick Hartwell, "Dialect Interferences in Writing," *Research in the Teaching of English,* XIV (May 1980), p. 109.

[19] Hartwell, pp. 109-110.

[20] Loren S. Barritt and Barry M. Kroll, "Some Implications of Cognitive-Developmental Psychology for Research in Composing," in *Research on Composing,* eds. Charles R. Cooper and Lee Odell (Urbana, Ill., 1978), pp. 53-54.

[21] Robert Michnick Golinkoff, "A Comparison of Reading Comprehension Processes in Good and Poor Comprehenders," *Reading Research Quarterly,* XI (1975-1976), pp. 623-659.

[22] Weaver, p. 18.

[23] Weaver, p. 17.

[24] Emig, p. 99.

Bibliography

Applebee, Arthur N. "Writing and Reading," *Journal of Reading,* XX (March 1977), pp. 534-537.

Bamberg, Betty. "Composition Instruction Does Make a Difference," *Research in the Teaching of English,* XII (February 1978), pp. 47-59.

Barritt, Loren S., and Barry M. Kroll. "Some Implications of Cognitive-Developmental Psychology for Research in Composing," in *Research on Composing.* eds., Charles R. Cooper and Lee Odell. Urbana, Ill.: National Council of Teachers of English, 1978, pp. 49-57.

Bernhardt, Bill. *Just Writing.* New York: Teachers & Writers, 1977.

Emig, Janet. *The Composing Processes of Twelfth Graders.* Urbana, Ill.: National Council of Teachers of English, 1971.

Farrald, Robert, and Richard Schamber. *A Diagnostic and Prescriptive Technique.* Sioux Falls, S.D.: ADAPT Press, 1973.

Golinkoff, Roberta Michnick. "A Comparison of Reading Comprehension Processes in Good and Poor Comprehenders," *Reading Research Quarterly.* XI (#4, 1975-1976), pp. 623-659.

Goodman, Kenneth S. "Linguistically Sound Research in Reading," in *Improving Reading Research,* eds. Roger Farr et al. Newark, Delaware: International Reading Association, 1976, pp. 89-100.

Hartwell, Patrick. "Dialect Interference in Writing," *Research in the Teaching of English,* XIV (May 1980), pp. 101-118.

Heilman, Arthur W. *Principles and Practices of Teaching Reading.* Columbus, Ohio: Charles E. Merrill Publishing Company, 1972.

Koch, Carl, and James M. Brazil. *Strategies for Teaching the Composition Process.* Urbana, Ill.: National Council of Teachers of English, 1978.

Moffettt, James. *Teaching the Universe of Discourse.* Boston: Houghton Mifflin Company, 1968.

Neman, Beth. *Teaching Students to Write.* Columbus, Ohio: Charles E. Merrill Publishing Company, 1980.

New York State Preliminary Competency Test in Writing *Manual for Administrators and Teachers.* New York State Education Department, 1979.

Rosen, Lois. "An Interview with Janet Emig," *English Journal,* LXVIII (October 1979), pp. 12-15.

Shaughnessy, Mina P. *Errors and Expectations.* New York: Oxford University Press, 1977.

Stanford, Gene, ed. *How to Handle the Paper Load.* Urbana, Il.: National Council of Teachers of English, 1979.

Weaver, Constance. *Grammar for Teachers.* Urbana, Ill.: National Council of Teachers of English, 1979.

Williams, Leon. "Toward a Realistic Teacher Workload," *English Journal,* LXVIX (May 1980), pp. 9-11.

WRITTEN COMPOSITION IN EARLY CHILDHOOD: A DEVELOPMENTAL PROCESS

Adelle Jacobs
CUNY - York College

Writing has become as important a focus of interest among educators in recent years as reading, alone, once was. The importance of the early years as foundational for later reading achievement has been widely acknowledged, and reading readiness, with its varying interpretations, has long been an accepted concept. We must be equally aware of the need for developing *writing readiness* as we now look to our programs for the teaching of writing, especially in the crucially important early childhood years.

What constitutes writing readiness? How can teachers help young children learn to express themselves verbally, and in writing? In early childhood it is not only skill development that is involved. It is also the developmental level of the child, since young children are different from older children in very basic ways, and in ways that have important implications for teaching.

Young children are pre-logical. Piaget calls them pre-operational (Piaget and Inhelder, 1969). They cannot think logically; they cannot think abstractly. Their thinking is determined by their own, personal perceptions of the world. They learn through activity and can only really understand what they, themselves, have experienced. Their level of thought and their concept development determine their use of language. Young children are egocentric -- they can only understand their own points of view. They cannot understand the points of view of others, and they simply assume that others understand them. If their verbal expressions, oral or written, sometimes seem incomplete or incoherent to the listener or the reader, it is because young children do not know that what is clear to them may be unclear to someone else. Children of five or six are legalistic and believe that rules must be followed, but they often cannot follow rules themselves. This would be as true for rules of writing as it is for classroom rules or rules of play. Young children are curious, eager for new experiences, and eager to learn. By the first or second grade, they will stick to tasks that they have chosen, or that they see as worthwhile, until they have completed them to their own satisfaction (Erickson, 1963). They may seem to have very short attention spans when engaged in busy work assignments or tasks which they find onerous. Their small muscles, such as those in the hand and fingers, are not yet well-developed, particularly at five or six years of age. Some young children find writing very fatiguing. Holding and controlling a pencil is a skill that will need time and practice and continuing development. Many children at these ages still do not have the perceptual skills necessary to distinguish the shapes of letters and do not have the eye-hand coordination to form the letters in writing. It is not unusual to find that they cannot tell left from right (Smart and Smart 1977).

Many chidren in kindergarten and first grade are not ready to write if, by writing, we mean using a pencil to make the marks that can be read by others. Writing readiness, like reading readiness, is a developmental state. It requires a foundation of oral language, perceptual skills, small muscle development, eye-hand coordination, the ability to tell left from right and an understanding that abstract marks on paper represent thoughts, feelings, and spoken words. Writing development depends, too on concept development which in turn, depends to some extent on maturation, but also on experience. A child needs experiences in order to have things to think about and to write about. Neither development nor readiness can be taught, but they can be facilitated, supported, and nurtured by good teachers.

Oral language is basic to writing. Five and six year olds come to school with large vocabularies, using the sentence structures and speech patterns of the languages heard in their home environments. As they mature and have new experiences, as they interact with children and adults at school, they develop increasing vocabularies and more complex syntactic forms to express their ideas and feelings. They need to be fluent and comfortable in the use of oral language in order to put their verbal skills to paper. The classroom should offer a rich and stimulating oral language environment. Children should talk with teachers and be talked with, individually and in small groups. Children should talk with each other freely. They should be encouraged to work together and share ideas, rather than to be silent. Children learn by doing. They learn to use language by using it. Children should play together. Symbolic play (role playing and dramatization) which begins in the earliest years, becomes more complex as children mature. It, too, is a form of symbolization in which ideas, feelings, and events are represented, and is especially conducive to the use of oral language.

Many interesting and varied experiences give children things to think about, to talk about, and to write about. Writing cannot happen in a vacuum. Children's experiences in the "real world" -- at home, with friends, their pets, perhaps their travels, as well as their fears and their pleasures -- provide opportunities for language that should be used to the maximum in school. School, too, must provide rich and interesting experiences. Sitting in their seats, silently attending to basal readers and workbooks will not inspire creative writing. Neighborhood walks, trips to places of interest, visitors in the classroom, pets, plants, good stories and poetry, cooking, and all of the subject areas of the curriculum provide content for thinking, feeling, and writing.

Even before children can write, they put ideas and feelings on paper when they paint or draw. Painting, drawing and writing serve similar functions -- they are all modes through which children portray their worlds, including details of importance, omitting what seems unimportant, sorting and clarifying their thoughts and feelings, assimilating reality, as Piaget would put it (Piaget and Inhelder 1969). They may also develop greater self-understanding and, perhaps, achieve emotional release in the process. In the early years, the drawing or the painting *is* the writing.

Before children can write they often, but not always, dictate a caption or a story to explain what they have painted or drawn. This should not be required of them, but they should have the opportunity to do so if they wish. However, drawing is important to written expression even into the grades (Emig 1977). The drawing process is a graphic expression of ideas and feelings, and as the child works these out in picture symbols, it facilitates putting the thoughts into verbal and written form (Platt 1977, Fillmer and Zepeda de Kane 1980, Hechinger 1979). So children should be drawing, even when they can write, and the graphic representation will pave the way for verbal expression.

Children often dictate simple, short stories if they have a teacher who is willing to act as scribe. The stories may be about anything that interests them -- Superman, Batman, cowboys, monsters, or an event that they may have experienced or fantasized. These may, but need not always, be related to their art work. As teachers take down their words, whether individual or group compositions, children learn that what is said can be written in symbols which can, in turn, be read over and over again. This is the next step in the development of both written expression and reading. Sometimes young children show their interest in writing by copying the text which the teacher has recorded for them. When they are able, they begin to write their compositions for themselves.

Young children need bridges to get to the state of writing readiness. Donald H. Graves calls *drawing* the "bridge from speech to print" (Hechinger 1979). Sara W. Lundsteen calls *dictation* "the major bridge to writing" (Lundsteen 1976). Both are good bridges, and both should be used.

When children begin to write they should of course, be encouraged to do so. But they still need the help of an adult when what they have to say is just more than they can handle with the limitations of their newly developing skill. Writing a story laboriously, letter by letter, can make even the most verbal and imaginative child feel that it is just too tedious and frustrating to be worth the effort. Prehaps this is especially true of the verbal and imaginative child, whose oral language fluency is far beyond his or her development in handwriting and spelling. So teachers must help get the ideas onto paper, acting as recorders for children in order to produce the written expression.

When children dictate to teachers, whether it is a group experience chart or an individual or group story, the language of the child, or children, should be used. Acceptance of their language is important. It is difficult for children to separate how they speak from who they are, and from their concepts of self. It is equally important to accept their ideas and the feelings they express. Children must feel that their lives are worth writing about and that what they have to say is interesting and of value. Negative comments and criticism only serve to put them on notice that it is dangerous to expose themselves and that the less they express, the safer they will be. Their written words are a statement of personal identity.

Developing written expression is a gradual process. It is fostered in a classroom climate in which children feel safe to express themselves. It is fostered by a teacher who is supportive and accepting, even when the expression of ideas, emotions, questions, and/or interests may, at times, be unusual or disturbing, or when the child uses language that makes the teacher uncomfortable. (Sylvia Ashton-Warner elicted such language from the Maori children she describes in *Teacher*.) Written expression is fostered by a teacher who does not make children self-conscious about -- or ashamed of -- their ideas, feelings, or language. As children have positive writing experiences they should come to feel that communicating ideas and emotions in writing is gratifying. Written expression is fostered by a teacher who enjoys the writing process and shows pleasure in the children's use of words and in the shared use of words.

Children should be encouraged to write for their satisfaction. A personal file or notebook may be kept for this purpose so that children may add to it daily, or several times a week. If their writings are truly personal expression, children should not be required to share them, but should be given the opportunity to do so if and when they choose. If they share their written work they learn that writing also serves to communicate ideas to others, as well as to record for oneself. Children often enjoy having books made of their writings. Individual stories or collections of work by one or more authors can have covers and be stapled or bound, to be kept by the child or placed in a classroom library.

Mechanical errors are not important in the kindergarten and the primary grades. Teachers may help children with these on an individual basis as children seem ready, but quality in writing comes with experience and maturation, and the help of good teachers, over time.

Young children should be free to use imagination, to choose their own topics, to find their own, unique ways of expressing themselves, to play with language, and to spell to their own satisfaction at least in personal papers. They should be permitted as much, or as little, time as they feel they need to express what they want to say. Topics may be suggested by the teacher, but should not be imposed. A child may choose not to write at all at a particular time, and that choice should be respected. We all have times like that, and writing should not be experienced as drudgery. The practice of assigning writing activities as punishment should be banished from classrooms where the development of creative writing and pleasure in writing are valued. Such assignments may or may not help to improve the behavior of children. They most assuredly help to develop negative feelings toward writing.

To assess a program for developing written composition in early childhood, *observe the children.* Are they eager to write? Do they have their own ideas regarding what they want to write about? Or do they depend on others for ideas? Do they seem engrossed in their writing? Do they show pleasure in their products? Do they seem to become more comfortable about writing with time and experience, or do they seem more hesitant with time? More inhibited? More reluctant? *Observe the curriculum.* Is the program rich in oral language, including literature, music and play? Are children encouraged to talk with each other and with the teacher? Are the graphic arts included as a basic ingredient of the curriculum? Do children have opportunities to dictate captions and stories before they are developmentally ready to write them themselves? Is the program rich in real and interesting experiences which may serve as referents for the children's thoughts and feelings? *Observe the classroom climate.* Does the teacher approach writing activities as a chore, or is there an air of anticipation and evidence of pleasure in the children's compositions? Is the classroom atmosphere supportive of children, of their thoughts, their feelings, their language, their experiences, and their attempts to put it all together in written form? These are the elements to look for, because they are the ones that make the difference in the development of written composition in the early childhood years.

Many thanks to the teachers and children of Public School #251, Queens, who shared their work with the author.

References

Almy, Millie; Chittendent, Edward; and Miller, Paula. *Young Children's Thinking: Studies of Some Aspects of Piaget's Theory.* New York: Teachers College Press, 1966.

Ashton-Warner, Sylvia. *Teacher.* New York: Simon and Schuster, 1963.

Emig, Janet. "Commentary: Learning to Write." *Language Arts* 54, 7 (October 1977) 739-40.

Erikson, Erik. *Childhood and Society,* 2nd ed. New York: W. W. Norton, 1963.

Fillmer, H. Thompson and Zepeda de Kane, Francis. "Drawing the Language Arts Together." *Language Arts* 57, 6 (September 1980) 640-642.

Ginsburg, Herbert and Opper, Sylvia. *Piaget's Theory of Intellectual Development.* Englewood Cliffs, N.J.: Prentice-Hall, 1969.

Hechinger, Fred M. "The Arts Termed Once of the 'Basics.'" *The New York Times,* May 1, 1979.

Lundsteen, Sara W. *Children Learn to Communicate.* Englewood Cliffs, N.J.: Prenctice-Hall, 1976.

Maier, Henry W. *Three Theories of Child Development.* New York: Harper and Row, 1969.

Platt, Penny. "Grapho-linguistics: Childen's Drawings in Relation to Reading and Writing Skills." *The Reading Teacher.* 31, 1 (December 1977) 262-268.

Smart, Mollie S. and Smart, Russell C. *Children: Development and Relationships,* 3rd ed. New York: Macmilan, 1977.

BUILDING A FICTIONAL WORLD: MOTIVATING WRITING THROUGH VARIETY

Terence D. Mosher
SUNY - Fredonia

For many writing teachers across New York State, these are nail-biting days. To the optional Regents Comprehensive Examination in English, whose thirty-point essay question has brought June jitters to several generations of senior-high English teachers, has been added the required Regents Competency Test in Writing, and both junior-high and elementary teachers of writing have joined the ranks of the uneasy, as eighth and ninth graders are taking the preliminary competency tests. Understandably, administrators are hoping that deficiencies in their schools' writing programs will not suddenly be laid bare by these exams. At every level, therefore, teachers are raising rather anxious questions like these: "Should I learn how to gear all of my teaching of writing toward the Competency Tests? And perhaps toward the Englsh Regents as well? Since so much rides on these exams, does a writing teacher have any other valid goals? Should I drop other aims and get on with 'teaching to the test'?"

Such an approach to teaching writing -- never intended by the State's test makers -- is not only grim for both students and teachers, but almost always futile. With rare exceptions, "teaching to the test" backfires when the test involves writing. Unless our schools are willing to settle for *only* minimal competency in their students' writing (and I am confident that they are not), they will need to broaden the present writing curriculum rather than narrow it.

Of course, a high-school junior who has written nothing but essays geared toward the two Regents exams may pass them both. In fact, he may do better than just pass. But he will probably never write a good essay. When it works, after all, the essay usually raids the other modes. The persuasive esay persuades by telling a hypothetical story to cement its point; in other words, it turns into fiction. The narrative essay breaks into dialogue, becoming for a moment a play. With playful bit of rhyme or a pleasing rhythm, a touch of poetry comes to the rescue of a potentially dry piece of description. Like the western rider who must try an English saddle to acquire a lighter touch and ride bareback to learn real balance, the student trying to learn the essay must also grapple with fiction and dialogue and many other modes of writing. The horse of composition demands a versatile rider that years of practice with straight expository prose can never train. As Richard Lanham puts it, if a student "is encouraged to write *only* this kind of . . . prose, he will *never write it at all.*"[1] Not, that is, with more than a bare minimum of competency that neither the student nor his teacher will find very satisfying, the very nature of writing, then, makes teaching entirely toward an essay exam almost hopeless. Still, there is plenty of hope in other directions.

Charles Cooper, co-editor of *Research on Composing: Points of Departure,* argues that, in order to help students grow as writers, a writing program must involve "writing often and in many modes." The modes of composition that Cooper believes all students should attempt and practice before high-school graduation are these:

dramatic writing (Moffett, 1968)
  dialogues - scenes -
    short plays (Hoetker and Engelsman, 1973)
  socratic dialogue
  dramatic monologue
  interior monologue

sensory recording
reporting (Moffett, 1968; Wiggington, 1972, 1973)
  observational visit
  interview
  reporter-at-large
  case study
  profile

generalizing and theorizing
  essay about the literary work (Roberts, 1969)

research
  (from lower-order, primary documents, not from

  textbooks, summary articles, or encyclopedias)

personal writing
 journal - diary - log
 personal letter
 autobiography
  (Moffett, 1968; Porter and Wolf, 1973)
 biography
 chronicle

poetry (Koch, 1970)

prose fiction
 utopias
 short stories (Moffett, 1968; Cooper, 1973)

business-practical (Brusaw and Alfred, 1973)
 personal resume and job application
 forms
 technical reports
 giving instructions
 explaining a process
 memo
 business letter
  communicating technical information
  requesting information
  transmitting a report[2]

A tall order for any ten writing teachers, let alone one? Not so tall, I think, if we spread repeated practice in these six major modes over the full twelve years of a student's education. As James Moffett demonstrates in *Student-Centered Language Arts and Reading, K-13,*[3] even first graders can do delightful work in several of these forms with the right sort of instruction and encouragement. If a full school system is unable to hammer out and implement a K-12 writing curriculm, Cooper's scheme can still be put to work by giving secondary English students practice in one new mode per year, beginning in grade seven, or two per year starting in grade ten. In short, Cooper's list looks long and utopian only to a teacher who must take his/her students through all of these modes alone, in the short space of a year or perhaps even a semester. To return to an earlier metaphor, this teacher's task is a bit like trying to turn a green weekend rider into a bronc buster, a barrel racer, a polo star, and a jockey, all in ten months' time.

For many secondary English teachers in New York State, however, this imaginary dilemma is a daily reality. In some high schools, textbook exercises and expository themes ARE the present writing curriculum. One or two teachers in such schools, aware that their students cannot grow without "writing often and in many modes," can only wonder where to start, or whether to bother starting at all. After all, at best they can offer their students only a sampling of Cooper's varied diet of writing tasks. They can count on no continuity for these students, who will soon move on to another teacher and more of the old expository-prose curriculum. And how will the students themselves react? Long since accustomed to an annual pilgrimage from phrase to clause to sentence to paragraph to what Janet Emig calls the five-part, "Fifty-Star Theme,"[4] how will such students respond to a teacher who begins with interior monologues and moves on to short stories and utopias? At first, so new an approach to what has always been a predictable process may threaten them.

But the risks invovled in Cooper's kind of curriculum may be its greatest strength. As Mary Beaven explains, those who take chances are often those who learn:

> Risk-taking, trying new behaviors as one writes, and stretching one's use of language and toying with its are important for growth in writing. Rogers (1962) describes the full-functioning person as one who prefers growth to safety seeking opportunities for "play" with perceptions, ideas, emotions, modes of expression, etc. According to Maslow (1962 and 1971), risk-taking is a trait of self-actualizing people, a trait which can be developed as teachers provide the necessary environment, opportunities, and interpersonal support. Maslow (1971) states that through participation in the creative arts people develop risk-taking abilities, becoming more fully-functioning; he argues that education should be centered on participation in creative expression in all the arts, writing included.[5]

The moral for the writing teacher seems clear. Learning to write well means trying out new voices, experimenting with new modes, addressing new audiences, and writing about new subjects. In short, it means being given the opportunity to take risks, to experience failures along with successes, and to learn from one's inevitable mistakes. Even if he/she must proceed with limited time, little cooperation from colleagues, and some occasional resistance from students, therefore, the writing teacher must somehow bring to the classroom the richly varied curriculum Charles Cooper has described. He/She needn't, of course, use Cooper's scheme. Like Cooper, the teacher must devise some reasonably orderly way to give his/her writing program real variety.

Granted, then that growth demands variety, how does a teacher DO all this? How does he/she keep the variety from becoming chaos? Finding a scheme such as Cooper's, does he/she begin with the first kind of writing and work down the list, stopping wherever he/she happens to be in January or June? Or does he/she give students several choices to topic and mode for each assignment they write? And can he/she somehow work all this practice in writing into the teacher of literature, or is that a wholly separate matter?

Before describing in some detail one manageable way to get started with a more diverse writing curriculum, I want to mention two other methods that I have seen used with considerable success. Some teachers, armed with James Moffett's *Teaching the Universe of Discourse* and its comprehensive structure of writing modes, begin in September with dramatic writing (interior monologue, soliloquy, short dialogue, full-length script), move on to several types of narrative (including letter and diary narration, memoir, and detached autobiography), and end with the essay (generalizing, theorizing, etc.).[6] In other words, they begin on the bottom rung of Moffett's ladder of abstraction and climb straight upward. Many teachers, though, soon run into problems as they climb. The first is time. Working with just a year or a semester, one has to omit many of Moffett's forms of discourse, and how does one choose the most important? The second problem is topic selection. Never having assigned an interior monologue or a diary narrative before, how does a teacher find sound and appealing topics for these assignments? Until he/she has some practice, this can be very difficult.

A second approach I have seen taken to the varied writing curriculum offers at least a partial solution to the eternal problem of choosing topics. Many teachers are finding that the literature they cover in class provides a ready-made stimulus to writing in a variety of voices and modes. Often with real excitement, their students are writing dialogues between Huck Finn and Holden Caulfield, keeping the diary Friar Laurence might have kept at the height of the suspense and intrigue in *Romeo and Juliet,* and trying their hand at fantasy stories in the *Hobbit* manner. Here, the teacher's great challenge is to plan and coordinate all this reading and writing smoothly, matching assignments to literary works in appropriate and challenging ways. Clearly, this is a handful the first time or two around.

Below, I describe a third way to begin diversifying a writing program. No better or worse in itself than the other two methods I have outlined, it does have some compelling advantages for both teachers and students who are new to this approach to composition. First, this method has built-in organization that makes planning and day-by-day execution relatively easy. Second, it is self-contained and needn't be coordinated with the literature program. Third, it all but eliminates the topic-choice problem, providing students themselves with both the responsibility and the means of choosing their own topics. Fourth, it can easily be used in a composition class (where up to a month can be devoted to it) or a regular English class (where it can best be handled through several one-week units, each one separated from the next by a few intervening weeks). Fifth, although it is designed mainly for senior-high English class, it can be reduced in scale for junior-high or even elementary students. Sixth, and most important, both students and teachers find it fun. Like every other writing activity, it works no miracles. But I have seen it elicit some good writing, bring some poorly motivated writers to life and improve the outlook of more than one teacher on the whole process of teaching composition.

As a visiting teacher at Maple Grove Junior-Senior High School in Bemus Point, New York, I first tested this project in a senior-high class in basic composition.

Although the class consisted mainly of average and below-average high-school writers, I did have two distinct advantages at Maple Grove. First, I was team-teaching the project with the class's regular teachers, Miss Carol Lucie. Second, Carol is a master teacher on whose marvelous rapport with her students and ability to motivate them I gratefully relied. Since this first experiment, however, I have seen the project repeated in a variety of forms by several other teachers who worked alone, and even by a few of the student teachers I have supervised in my work at Fredonia State College. Neither team-teaching nor extensive experience, then, are necessary to make the project work.

The project itself, which I shall describe through a past-tense account of the procedure we followed at Maple Grove and the reactions of our students, rests squarely on one assumption: most adolescents come to school as practiced veterans in the art of inventing fictional worlds. Nearly every American girl, after all, has built an extensive make-believe world around her dolls. Like the virtuoso actresses who play a dozen or more parts in one-woman shows, most little girls play fictional games in which they take on the voices of every member of their doll families, from the brat to the bully to the beautiful, sweet Cinderella, playing each part with ease. Meanwhile, the neighborhood boys move happily through the worlds of the space fantasy, the western, and the crime drama, taking the parts of one TV superhero after another. It is so common, this ability to take on voices, that we scarcely notice it, but still it is no mean accomplishment. And in various forms it continues into adolescence. Simply to get through a day without offending others, most high-school students must play a wide variety of roles as their discourse moves from subject to subject and audience to audience. The junior fullback, e.g., probably has a locker-room voice (or several of them) for his teammates and a guidance-office voice for Miss Fidditch, who loves football but blanches at locker-room rhetoric. In the same way, his language and manner are likely to change sharply when his father moves the topic of conservation from last night's game to last night's indiscretion behind the wheel of the family car. Thus, if the adolescent's old childhood habit of inventing more or less complete fictional worlds has usually waned by the time he or she reaches high school, the role playing that is so much a part of these worlds simply persists in a different, more functional form. The writing project I shall describe tries to exploit on paper the adolescent's rather remarkable facility as a role player. At the same time, it tries to reawaken some of the old joy in creating and living within a fairly complete, systematic world of make-believe, a world with invented characters, plot, and at least the rudiments of theme.

As a stimulus to fiction-making, we first asked Carol's class to read this poem from Stephen Dunning's *Mad, Sad, and Glad,* a fine collection of verse and photography by high-school students:

THE FUNERAL

Part I

so there we were
at Tex and Bogie's
and everybody was keeping their
cool
even the bereaved
and even though we
were there for a funeral
it was kinda nice seeing all
those people again
till Hazel came
and said it couldn't have
happened at a worse
time
well god damn
what are we supposed to do
"a pardon me Hazel
I was wondering if
it's alright with you
if Johnny dies this week
I mean if you're not busy
or something"
but we just love her to
come and tell us
all about her operation
and her daughter's divorce
and really cheer us up.

Part II

the shroud wasn't anywhere near the
deceased
it fell on us as the time got near
funny how a guy's name changes
as soon as he dies
no longer is he Johnny
or John
or Buster
or any of the names
he ever had
now he's the deceased
just that

        Kevin Bales
        Ponca City Senior High School
        Ponca City, Oklahoma
        1970[7]

In class, we talked first about the narrator's winsome, sensitive voice, about the not-so-sensitive Hazel, and about the power of names and nicknames to control our perceptions of people. Next, Carol and I asked the class to consider some questions the poem is silent about, questions it invites us to answer out of our own imaginations. First, who's talking to us here? A teenage friend of Johnny's? A young cousin, perhaps? Or does the narrator's easy-going diction ("keeping their cool") have to be the language of a teenager at all? The class turned at once into a debate, orderly and chaotic by turns. Some argued violently that a fourteen-year-old would be fully capable of the sober reflections in stanza two, while others said that those were clearly the thoughts of an adult. Still others decided that the poem changes speakers in the second stanza: some other guest at Tex and Bogie's, they felt, takes over here, giving the same poem two different speakers. The class disagreed just as vigorously over the questions, "Who was Johnny?" Many opted for a high-school junior or senior, but a few devil's advocates almost convinced them that Johnny dies an old man, known to his dying day as "Buster" by a devoted wife. For the most part, Carol and I just stood back and enjoyed the fun. Next came a debate over what sort of place "Tex and Bogie's" was. The home of Johnny's parents? A relative's home, perhaps? Not content with our tame speculations, one class comedian announced that Tex and Bogie's was the town funeral parlor, where a flashing neon sign proclaimed the names of the proud proprietors. Several others (who nearly carried the day) insisted on a bar run by friends of Johnny. Johnny's family and friends, they argued, had gathered there not for the funeral itself, but for a celebration in honor of his memory.

Sharing and enjoying these ideas -- from the most thoughtful and logical to the most whimsical and frivolous -- was an important pre-writing activity. First, it gave the whole project an open, spirited, experimental atmosphere from the start, dispelling any notions that there might be a "best" way to go about it that Carol and I would be "looking for" as the project moved along. Second, it was our first practice in building fictional worlds. As they began to surround Johnny with a variety of possible friends, relatives, places, and events, students began to discover what fun such worlds can be to invent and to live in.

After a day of this zany experimentation, Carol and I insisted that the class agree upon a fixed cast of about fifteen characters who might have lived in Johnny's world. Some, we said, should be his friends and close relatives. Others should be more distant acquaintances or people who knew Johnny in roles such as teacher, minister, or storekeeper. Finally, a few should enter the world in official capacity connected with Johnny's death, funeral, or burial. If they wished, the class could include Tex and Bogie, the narrator, and Hazel in their cast. This process of agreeing upon a set of coherently related characters took about one class period and revived many f the debates of the previous day. At times, we simply ad to quash these and, asking the class to vote, decide whether Johnny was 18 or 45, whether Hazel was his great aunt or girlfriend, and whether he had a best friend or brother who should be added to the cast of characters. As the cast took shape, Carol and I listed the characters' names and a few facts about each one on the blackboard.

At the same time, we had to agree upon the outlines of a plot. Very quickly, the class realized that we couldn't choose many of our "official" characters -- those with some professional role to play in the events surrounding Johnny's death -- without agreeing upon how he died. Having decided to make Johnny a high-school student of 18 growing up in a small Oklahoma town, the class seized upon a motorcycle crash as the cause of his untimely death. Inspired, I suspect, by the multiplying misfortunes of soap-opera characters and the melodramatic deaths of old rock-song heroes like the late, lamented "Leader of the Pack," they decided in the space of one minute that Johnny had fought with his girlfriend, gotten deeply depressed, mixed drugs and alcohol, and, scarcely aware of what he was doing, ridden his huge and famous motorcycle straight into an oncoming "semi" truck. Not a terribly promising plot. But this rather morbid and hackneyed choice of events opened the way for some interesting characters to join the cast. One was a tough, crusty old policeman who had always like Johnny in spite of his minor troubles with the law. Knowing that Johnny's was an unhappy home, this man had become a second father to him. When this policeman was called to the scene of Johnny' death, his reaction was a moving one. Out of a trite, rather insensitive choice of plot, then, came a character of some complexity and depth, sensitively conceived. Over and over again as the project progressed, this sort of thing happened. It is bound to happen, in fact, to anyone who invites young people to create fictional worlds. When twenty adolescent imaginations are given their head in one room, seriousness occasionally gives way to silliness. But no teacher should be discouraged by this pattern. The sillier moments are often hilarious, and part of our purpose in teaching writing is surely to show our students that composition isn't always a grim business. Before long, moreover, either naturally or with a bit of gentle prodding, silly ideas often lead back to serious ones.

Once the class had decided upon the full cast of characters, we assigned the project's first writing exercise: a one-page description of each character. Unlike many a descriptive essay I have assigned, this was one that many students couldn't wait to write. When we asked for a volunteer to describe each character, there was fair amount of competition for favorites like Harriet Wodazzeedo, Johnny's 84 year-old English teacher, and his Neanderthal football teammate Bronco Brown. Students liked this assignment, I think, for several reasons. First, they knew that each description would be mimeographed and given to the rest of the class, and publication often boosts motivation. Second, since the characters were their own collective creation, they were already fond of them and anxious to make them into colorful, memorable people. Finally, they knew that each description would wield considerable clout during the rest of the project: their classmates would be writing about these characters and trying to capture their distinctive voices, and we should insist that all this writing be faithful to the original descriptions.

We gave the class two days to write, edit, and recopy on ditto masters their descriptions of the charaters. As they drafted and thought, we moved around the classroom offering help. Both then and during the rest of the project, part of this help consisted simply of reading what students had written so far and saying at least one postive thing about it. Needless to say, we were occasionally reduced to praising penmanship. But nothing seemed to generate good work like an enthusiastic "Great!" or a laugh over some witty touch.

To help students expand and refine their drafts, we gave a second kind of assistance. Rather than point to specific faults in a piece or prescribe specific changes, we tried to ask questions that might help a writer consider new ways to approaching his subject. Most of these questions we borrowed from Lee Odell, co-editor of *Evaluating Writing: Describing, Measuring, Judging* and designer of a set of intellectual strategies for writers that have proven extremely effective in the classroom. A few of the questions we found useful were these: Can you place your character in a physical context? Where would you be likely to find him? Where would you never find him? What friends or acquaintances of yours is he like? Which ones is he unlike? How is he like you? Or different from you? How is he like or unlike characters you know of in literature or television or the movies? How, if at all, has he changed in his life so far? How might he be changed by Johnny's death?[8] What are his distinctive quirks of personality and/or appearance? What was his relationship to Johnny like? His relationships to the other characters?

Quite often, as we slowly raised these questions and a student mulled each one over, a light bulb would suddenly seem to light and he/she would send us off to the next writer with a remark like, "Ah! I just realized what I want to say next." At first, the bulbs took some time to light. Eventually, though, the class grew quite adept at answering our questions and, in some cases, at raising them on their own. Especially for these students, writing became a somewhat more deliberate and manageable process.

The character descriptions themselves were no masterpieces, but still interesting and lots of fun. As always, there were some straight stereotypes. Miss Wodazzeedo, wrote her creator, was certain that Johnny took his own life "to get out of an English report" and felt secretly relieved to hear of his demise because "she had twenty chairs and twenty-one students." Scarcely a kind description, but scarcely serious, either. The writer had great fun making her outrageous. Johnny's high school principal received the same heavy-handed ironic treatment, improved a bit by hints of Dickensian grotesquery. "After the last bell rings," began the description, "the principal drags along the lonely coridors with his stiff left leg and his crooked cane, searching for wrongdoings."

Many characters, of course, fared better. Officer Crumky, the policeman whose description I summarized above, turned out to be a much more sympathetic, intricate character than his name might suggest. And even Hazel, first described stereotypically as "a sophisticated, stuck-up snob" whose chief aim in life was impressing others with expensive clothes and perfume costing $50 an ounce, was allowed a touch of sympathy. Because of her staggering clothing bills, she lived in near-poverty in a shabby three-room house, reaping every day the fruits of her vanity. However fantastic and far-fetched, Hazel could never be called a dull lady. As the project moved along, students found that, like most of the other characters, she was fun to write about.

For the next four weeks, the class lived in the fictional world they had built, peopling it with the characters they had described. As we moved from week to week at Maple Grove High, time also moved forward in Johnny's Oklahoma town. First came the week before Johnny's death, a period of "business as usual" in his family, community, and school. Our second week on the project corresponded to the week of Johnny's death; each character learned of the tragedy and reacted in a characteristic way. Third came the week of Johnny's funeral; in which every member of the cast was somehow involved. In our last week in Johnny's world, his family and friends tried to pick up their lives and, in their very different ways, cope with Johnny's sudden absence.

We divided the class into four writing groups of about four students apiece, using the same groups throughout the project. (In larger classes, writing groups of six or seven have worked well.) Every week, each group would try a different kind of composition. By the end of the project, each group had experienced these four modes of writing:

1. JOURNALISM, including news, sports, feature articles, and advertisements from the local paper in Johnny's town, a variety of articles from his high-school newspaper, and features in his class yearbook.
2. PERSONAL WRITING, including the notes, letters, and diary entries written by different members of the cast of characters during the month surrounding Johnny's death.
3. DRAMATIC WRITING, including the interior monologues (for thoughts), the monologues (or speeches), and the dialogues (or conversations) of the whole cast as they reacted to the events of these four weeks.
4. OFFICIAL OR PROFESSIONAL WRITING, such as the policeman's official report on Johnny's accident, the coroner's death certificate, and the eulogy delivered by Johnny's minister.

The writing done by any group during a particular week, then always depended upon two factors: 1. which of the four modes of writing (above) the group was working with, and 2. what stage we had reached in our four-week plot, i.e., what was happening in Johnny's world during that week. For example, during the project's second week, the week of Johnny's death, the group writing journalism might concentrate on local news articles about the accident and the ensuing investigation, announcements concerning the time and place of the funeral, editorials about drug abuse or teenage driving and pieces in the school newspaper about the sorrow and shock suffered by Johnny's classmates and teachers. During the following week, a different group would be writing a different sort of journalism. Since it would now be the week of the funeral, the local paper might carry an account of the service and burial, excerpts from the eulogy, and announcements of scholarships or memorial funds to be raised in Johnny's name. The school newspaper might carry a long tribute to Johnny with an account of his full school career and some interviews with his family, teachers, and friends. By the beginning of the project's second week, i.e., after we had moved the plot ahead for the first time and assigned a new kind of writing to each of the four writing groups, this organization was clear to everyone. The project's day-by-day organization, described below, was also easy to follow.

MONDAY: PREWRITING DAY. Every Monday, Carol and I would assign each group a new kind of writing to work with over the next week, and as a class we would review the events taking place in Johnny's world that week. Then, with an occasional suggestion from us, each group would discuss possible pieces of writing it might produce, and a chairperson would assign each member of the group a specific piece to write by Thursday of that week. The group would then make suggestions to help each writer get started. In the group writing journalism, e.g., it might be decided that Mike would write a straight news account of the accident, Karen a follow-up story on the reactions of Johnny's family, and Bill a letter to the editor attacking the legal drinking age as the cause of the tragedy. Meanwhile, the group doing dramatic writing might ask Jim to write a dialogue between the policeman and Johnny's father when the news of Johnny's death was broken, and Mary might be assigned a very different dialogue taking place the next day between Johnny's football coach and the high-school principal. In most cases, these planning sessions were lively and fun. Students seemed to enjoy playing with possibilities and usually came away excited about what they would write.

TUESDAY AND WEDNESDAY: WRITING DAYS. As Carol and I moved around the room, encouraging and questioning in the ways described above, students drafted and revised the pieces they had been assigned in Monday's planning sessions. Since they generally liked what they were writing, these were relaxed, pleasant days.

THURSDAY: EDITING DAY. If he/she hadn't done so already, each writer showed a draft to one of three student editors, who helped edit it for basic mechanical and stylistic problems. Next the drafts were recopied on ditto masters and mimeographed. On this busy day, Carol and I helped with both the editing and the dittoing, which was done in a faculty workroom and required some active policing.

FRIDAY: SHARING DAY. The best day of all. On one Friday, we simply passed out the dittoed material and let everyone read it all. Before long, someone was in hysterics over a disciplinary lecture by Miss Wodazzeedo, and someone else was sincerely praising a moving argument between Johnny's two sisters, one of them devoted to him and the other indifferent, over who should move into his old room. Quite spontaneously, the compliments went on for most of the period. On another Friday, Carol and I took turns reading excerpts from each piece, inviting the class to comment on its strengths. Once, we asked volunteers to read what they had written that week, and the highlight of the day was a pair of eulogies, one a rollicking parody, the other more serious and, in spots, quite moving.

Of course, we expected and received no pieces that were ready for publication in *The New Yorker*. Working almost entirely with new modes of writing, our students had no choice but to learn by making mistakes. With dramatic writing, e.g., nearly everyone had the typical beginner's problem with erratic diction, so that the same character in a dialogue might sound like a courtier one moment and a grease monkey the next. Casual notes and letters sometimes read like formal essays, and certain kinds of professional jargon eluded our students compltely. Still, many of their pieces had real strengths. Few were dull. And the project's main aims were accomplished. Within an organized but flexible structure, every student wrote on a variety of topics, for a number of different audiences, and in a wide range of voices and modes. Stretching everyone's use of language, the project invovled extensive experimentation and risk-taking. While there were a few protests ("I can't do that -- I never even tried it before!"), most students welcomed the new challenges, and even the least motivated of them saw that writing could, after all, be fun.

Although the writing they did was too varied to become boring, students did get tired of living in the same fictional world and said they would have enjoyed the project more if we had given them a long break about halfway through it. For this reason, I think the following variation on the project would work well in a standard English 11 or 12 class, even with a traditional writing curriculum. A cast of characters, a place, and a basic plot could easily be created, then shelved, and periodically taken out and dusted off to provide speakers and topics for various writing assignments. Instead of wracking their brains for descriptive essay topics, e.g., teachers could have their students describe people and/or places from the fictional world. When a unit on persuasive writing rolls around, they could assign editorials or letters to the editor that might appear in the fictional town's newspapers. And a story-writing unit could involve stories about people and events in the imaginary world, as narrated by characters in the cast.

In the junior-high and elementary school, the project can be used on appropriately reduced scales, or tailored to different curricula and teaching styles. One eighth-grade English teacher whom I know, e.g., divided her classes into small groups and had each group generate a cast of characters, describe these characters in short essays, and then script and perform a mystery play involving the full cast. Complete with music, costumes, and props, the performances were delightful. In one elementary classroom, students were first asked to write descriptions of the characters in the nursery rhyme "Hey Diddle Diddle," in which a cow jumps over the moon and dish and a spoon elope. Having done this, the children added more characters of their own to the original cast. Finally, they began writing a variety of light, playful asignments such as the dish's love letter to the spoon and the moon's dialogue with the cow as she sails merrily overhead. As these classroom experiences suggest, if a teacher wishes to bring new variety to his present writing program, he can probably adapt the project I have described in a way that will make this possible. Above all, it is designed to be flexible.

REFERENCES

[1] Richard A. Lanham, *Style: An Anti-Textbook* (New Haven: Yale University Press, 1974), p. 67.

[2] Charles R. Cooper, "Measuring Growth in Writing," *English Journal* 64 (March 1975): 113.

[3] James Moffett, *Student-Centered Language Arts and Reading K-13* (Boston: Houghton Mifflin Company, 1976), Chaps. 14-16.

[4] Janet Emig, *The Composing Processes of Twelfth Graders*, NCTE Research Report No. 13 (Urbana, Ill.: National Council of Teachers of English, 1971), p. 97.

[5] Mary H. Beaven, "Individualized Goal Setting, Self-Evaluation, and Peer Evaluation," in *Evaluating Writing: Describing, Measuring, Judging,* ed. Charles Cooper and Lee Odell (Urbana, Ill.: National Council of Teachers of English, 1977), p. 137.

[3] James Moffett, *Teaching the Universe of Discourse* (Boston: Houghton Mifflin Co., 1968), p. 47.

[7] Kevin Bales, "The Funeral," in *Mad, Sad, and Glad,* ed. Stephen Dunning (New York: Scholastic Book Services, 1970), pp. 61-62.

[3] Lee Odell and Joanne Cohick, "You Mean, Write It Over in Ink?" *English Journal* 64 (December 1975); 51.

THE COMPOSING PROCESS AND ITS RELATIONSHIP TO THE TEACHING OF WRITING

Robert W. Blake

SUNY - College at Brockport

The composing process is not only related to writing. It *is* writing. I'll go even further. To paraphrase a competitor I admire a great deal, the composing process isn't *everything* to do with writing; it's the *only* thing.

If you want to teach writing, then you need to do a lot of writing yourself, different kinds of writing in different modes for different audiences. You need to analyze what you do as you compose; then you need to arrange what you do in the writing classroom to reflect this internalized knowledge about how people compose with words. If you don't follow some sort of process like this, you will be needlessly frustrated as you set out to discover how to teach others to write well.

Understanding Composing in Writing

Why do you need to understand the composing process? Most importantly, if you know about the stages in composing, this knowledge will help to dispel myths about writing.

Many textbooks on writing state or imply that to write, you must first make a detailed outline, find out exactly and completely what you want to say, and simply write out what you now know. But experienced writers tell you this isn't at all what they do. E. M. Forster, the novelist, made this now classic statement about how with him knowledge didn't precede writing but followed it. "How do I know what I think until I see what I say?" John Updike, the novelist and poet, put it this way: "Writing and re-writing are a constant search for what one is saying." And William Stafford, the poet, describes how his writing is discovery, not simply writing out what he already knows. "I don't see writing as communication of something already discovered, as 'truths' already known. Rather, I see writing as a job of experiment. It's like a discovery job; you don't know what's going to happen until you try it!" (cited in Murray, 1978, p. 103).

I'm aware that the writers I've marshalled to support my point write chiefly poetry and fiction, what we traditionally call "creative writing". Isn't that quite different from the types of writing we teach in the school classrooms, those being chiefly expository and persuasive? It surely is, but the fact remains that writers of exposition and writers of fiction and poetry describe composing in a similar way. Here, for instance, is a college writing teacher, Peter Elbow, in his provocative and useful little book, *Writing without Teachers,* explaining the composing process in writing. Says Elbow:

> The commonsense, conventional understanding is as follows: Writing is a two-step process. First you figure out your meaning, then you put it into language.... This idea of writing is backwards. That's what causes so much trouble.... Only at the end (of writing) will you know what you want to say or the words you want to say it with. You should expect yourself to end up somewhere different from where you started. *Meaning is not what you start out with but what you end up with.* (Italics mine) (pp. 14-15)

That statement is the exact opposite of the traditional notion of writing. But what Elbow and the others say about writing is true. People--students included--do write to discover meaning.

What, then, is the composing process in writing? How do we use it as the basis for a writing program in the schools?

In general terms, composing in writing--like composing in drawing, painting, or music--is a complex process in which thinking, feeling, and performing a physical act, like handwriting or typing, are all interrelated. Janet Emig makes a convincing case for the crucial connection among the hand, eye, and brain (1978). During the composing process, while the writer's hand, eyes and brain interact to produce a piece of writing, the writer, like someone playing three-dimensional chess, needs to keep in mind virtually simultaneously the key elements of message, audience, writer's role, focus, and structure, while, at the same time, she or he moves forward as well as backwards, sometimes circling with words, sentences, and larger structures, in which the unconscious mind may be as influential as the conscious intellect, acts leading to a piece which the writer many times may not be able to explain until she or he has worked completely through a draft. Indeed, the composing process is so complex and mysterious and yet, in many apparent ways, such a natural human process, that some individuals hold simply that writing is thought made visual by written symbols. Supporting this notion, James Moffett defines writing as the revision of an individual's inner speech and quite flatly states that writing "is nothing less than thinking" (1979, p. 278).

Stages in the Composing Process

There are many schemes for describing the composing process. In her seminal study of how senior high school students write, *The Composing Processes of Twelfth Graders,* Janet Emig describes these stages: 1. Context of Composing, 2. Nature of Stimulus, 3. Prewriting, 4. Planning, 5. Starting, 6. Composing Aloud (a special stage related to her study), 7. Reformulation, 8. Stopping and 9. Contemplation of Product (1971). Donald Murray identifies Prevision, Vision, and Revision (1978). James Britton labels these stages in the process: Conception, Incubation and Production (1975). There are other descriptions, of course, but I have found for the purposes of school instruction the following scheme to be simple, fairly accurate, and readily understood by both students and teachers. My categories are Prewriting, Drafting, Revising, and Editing.

Even though we label stages in the composing process and know something about what they are like, it doesn't mean we fully understand what goes on during these stages. For instance, the subconscious mind may have a far greater role to play during writing than most people--other than professional poets and novelists-- realize. Let me explain what I mean.

If we review the work done by neurosurgeons, psychiatrists, and psychologists, as reported in the general literature dealing with what is commonly called "right-left brain research," we find information about the workings of the human brain, which, in turn, teaches us how people create in writing. Robert Ornstein, one of the interpreters of this research, presents in his book, *The Psychology of Consciousness,* a review of the findings of right and left brain hemisphere operation (1972).

According to Ornstein, our brains are divided into two parts. The left hemisphere controls the right side of the body, the right hand, so to speak, and it deals with those mental activities we might label as *intellectual.* The operations include analyzing and thinking logically, especially with words and mathematical symbols, and handling information sequentially. States Ornstein: "This mode of operation of necessity must underly logical thought, since logic depends upon sequence and order. Language and mathematics, both left-hemisphere activities, also depend predominantly on linear time" (p. 67).

The right hemisphere, on the other hand, controls the left side of the body, the left hand, to continue the metaphor, and is responsible for activities we might label as *intuitive.* This right hemisphere handles information, not in a sequence, but appears to grasp reality all at once, as a whole. Ornstein describes the activities of the right hemisphere as learning with the "left hand": "If the left hemisphere can be termed predominantly analytical and sequential in its operation, then the right hemisphere is more holistic and relational, and more simultaneous in its mode of operation" (p. 68).

That's what men of science say about two general functions of parts of the brain dealing with language. Such an observation is amazing enough, but what is more uncanny is that experienced writers report that when they write, they go through mental stages which are strikingly like the two modes of consciousness pictured by the scientists. Too many writers to be discounted talk about at least two distinctly different stages in the composing process. The first, they report, is unconscious, personal, irrational, intuitive, the stage of thinking, meditating, recreating dreams, of producing a first draft without concern for mechanics, of relying on their individual muse or daemon or personal inner voice to lead them in writing where it will. After this initial, subconscious stage when the "left hand" is in control, the "right hand" takes over. Once they have produced the first draft, the writers then become conscious, impersonal, rational, and intellectual, as they revise the words which originally seemed to pour out of them.

Experienced writers describe what they do after they have moved through the prewriting stages and have a draft before them. F. Scott Fitzgerald, in notes made when he was writing *The Great Gatsby,* reported that he wrote out by hand the entire first draft of the novel and then set out to revise it, line by line, word by word. In a recent advertisement for International Paper Company on "How to Write with Style," Kurt Vonnegut says this about revising: "*Have the guts to cut....* Your rule might be this: Be merciless on yourself. If a sentence, no matter how excellent, does not illuminate your subject in some new and useful way, scratch it out" (1980).

We know, then, what experienced writers do as they follow through the stages of the composing process. If you write a lot yourself, and, after you have written, analyze what you do as you move from an idea or image to a finished piece of writing, I'm confident you'll discover you're following the same sort of process.

What do you do to help your students use the process as they write? First, you need to make them aware of the stages. The first stage of writing, you might tell them, is a period of "incubation" or "gestation," quite literally a time before birth, a time for seeing an image in a dream, a time for developing seemingly unrelated ideas and feelings into a plan, however tentative, for first draft writing. Throughout this stage, writers draw upon their knowledge, past experience, and relations with human beings and with other creatures as the raw material for a draft.

During this stage, encourage your students to rely on their personal, creative powers, trusting that one word will lead to another. To help them comprehend this step, make available to them quotes like this one by William Stafford:

> To get started I will accept anything that occurs to me... If I put down something, that thing will help the next thing come, and I'm off. If I let the process go on, things will occur to me that were not in my mind when I started. These things, odd or trivial as they may be, are somehow connected. And if I let

them string out, surprising things will happen. (p. 44)

Go on to point out that experienced writers spend as much as forty to fifty percent of their time for pieces with the prewriting stage and that they should not expect things to go much differently for them.

Once they have an idea of this stage, you need to supply them with situations for prewriting in the classroom. The following are some activities I've found useful at different times.

Activities for the Prewriting Stage

1. *Free Writing.* Use free writing with your students to get them started with the physical act of writing, which in turn tends to trigger more writing. For Peter Elbow, the "most effective way...to improve your writing is to do free writing exercises regularly. At least three times a week" (p. 3). With free writing, your students take pencil to paper and start writing anything that comes to mind for a specific period of time, from ten to fifteen minutes. Don't let them stop for anything during the period, not even to think about a particular word. If they can't think of the right one, then they may leave a blank. Certainly they are not to check **correct** spellings or bother with punctuation. And, of course, make it clear you're not going to grade this free writing.

The idea of free writing is simply to get the student moving the pencil across the paper until an image, idea, or even a pattern of ideas appears; the image, idea, or pattern then becomes something for the student to continue writing about.

Free writing is not all there is to writing instruction. It's only a specialized technique for getting people started.

2. *Remembering.* Encourage your students to cultivate their memories, to rely upon their past experiences as the single richest and most important storehouse of raw material from which to draw for writing. They need to be trained, as experienced writers have trained themselves, to extract this raw material from their minds, like a miner digging gold nuggets from deep in the earth. Or a better simile might be that the memory is like a subterranean lake of clear fresh, life-giving water, an almost limit-

less pool from which ideas and feelings continue to flow.

Here are questions for them to ask themselves.

What was my earliest memory?

What was my first house like? What's my chief image of my house?

What do I remember most about my mother, my father?

What did I fear the most as a child, love the most?

3. *Asking and Answering Questions.* Try to get your students used to listening to what they have to say to themselves, to have them make their inner voices external through words. Have them learn literally to talk to themselves, probing their memories and minds with questions about their ideas or feelings.

Is this what I mean?

What else should I include?

Is this logical? Does this make sense? What else should I know about this?

4. *Noticing How Things Change.* A fundamental technique for learning about the world is noting how things change.

How did my friend that I want to write about change over the last few months when her parents were being divorced?

How has my family changed? My town or city?

How has the treatment of women changed in the last ten years?

5. *Contrasting.* We learn about one thing by contrasting it with something else.

In what specific ways is this different from that?

How is junior high different from senior high? Soccer from football?

How do the roles of men and women differ in our society?

6. *Reading and Taking Notes.* Reading and reacting to what you read by jotting down notes on the reading is a time-honored means of interacting with another mind, with getting your ideas to bounce off the words of another. Students should get used to reading newspapers, magazines, pamphlets, and books for new positions dealing with topics they want to write about. It's useful for them to outline and summarize the ideas they find,

chiefly so they'll understand them, but sometimes they need to make personal and critical comments as well on their reading.

That doesn't sound right to me.
I wonder where she got that idea.
Boy, is this writer biased.

7. *Writing Dialogue.* Have your students write dialogue. Dialogue is, of course, necessary for fiction, but dialogue can also be used to articulate varied points of view on a controversial issue, to help students become sensitive to differing points of view, and to assist them in learning how to turn formal, academic prose into lively and immediate speech.

8. *Role Playing and Recording What Happens.* An extension of writing dialogue. People assume roles--usually conflicting--and spectators record what they say.

9. *Playing with Sentence Frames and Other Language Structures.* Such formal frames help students to gather and order details. Here is one kind of useful frame, employed successfully by Kenneth Koch for teaching school children to write poetry (1970).

I used to be _____, but now I am _____.

10. *Brainstorming.* With brainstorming, individuals say words related to a given topic--or to the words said--as fast as they can, while someone writes down what is reported. After the list of details is recorded, students may find a direction to the brainstormed words.

Remind your students that during this prewriting stage they may want to write just to find out the ideas and images which appear on paper. They will probably plan in some way before a first draft by making a scratch outline or by jotting down a short list of points. Whatever they do, they don't need a fullblown outline with heads and subheads. All experienced writers--sometimes before they start a draft and sometimes after they have written freely in order to find directions for a draft--do gather images, explore feelings, and order ideas; your students need to accept this preparation.

Writing the First Draft. Whatever has happened during the prewriting stage, the writing of the first draft is an often frightening and intimidating time for the inexperienced writer. You should let your students know you accept this. Your major aim at this level is to provide an atmosphere supportive enough so the students will have removed for them as many roadblocks as possible, so they can get some words down on paper, even though they know in the backs of their minds that what they have written--ideas, openings, endings, or even entire pages-- may change dramatically before the piece is completed. In a practical sense, you need to be there, like a long distance running coach or swimming coach, cheering your runners and swimmers on simply to finish the course.

No matter how experienced at writing they become, your students--like all other writers--will always feel the stark terror of a blank page. If they are to become effective writers, though, they must get used to that sense of dread, and, rather than being paralyzed by it, go beyond the feeling to finish a draft.

Janet Emig advances three substantial reasons why writing out by hand a first draft is so crucial to the composing process (1977). First, the physical act of writing appears to trigger ideas and images--the raw material of language--from the brain. Second, the crafting of words on paper--like painting or drawing--gives some writers aesthetic pleasure. And third, we need to write out a first draft because that's the only way a part of our brain works, by stringing out words one after another on a page. We write out a first draft simply because that is how, as human beings, we must do it.

The decision to start writing a first draft may be likened to that moment when a well-trained athlete makes the decision to start competition. Have you ever watched a high jumper or pole vaulter as he or she decides to commit himself to action? Much like a finely tuned athlete, the writer must meditate, psyche himself or herself up, gather all his or her internal forces, and then make the decision to go for it, to start writing.

Phillip Lopate says that teaching our students this feeling of inner readiness, of knowing how to listen to one's own "energy voice," of recognizing this "absolute moment to write," of feeling ready to begin writing, may very well be the most important thing about writing we can teach them (1978). In fact, for Lopate, once we know inside that we are at that moment to start writing, we have probably solved two-thirds of the technical problems--focus, structure, beginning, ending--with a piece.

How can you help beginning writers prepare themselves for starting and completing the first draft? Essentially, based upon the experiences they have had with the **drafting stages, they need to be able literally to talk them**selves through this stage, giving themselves pep talks and compelling themselves to keep on writing in spite of the quite normal gut feeling that what they're hacking away at is, without a doubt, the lousiest thing ever put down on paper. They must know, however, that they must pass through the first draft stage of lousy writing if they are ever going to produce anything worthwhile.

Here is advice they might give themselves during the frustration of the first draft.

Advice for Writers To Give Themselves During the First Draft

1. *Having Words Bounce Off Each Other.* Elbow calls the process of playing off ideas against summing up what the ideas seem to mean "cooking" (p. 73). If your students appear to have trouble with the balance between writing out words and thinking about what they mean, have them alternate the two activities. They can write for ten minutes and then sit back and see how what they wrote adds up. They might talk to themselves like this.

> Now that I've written that, let's see if I can find out what it means.
> What was I trying to say here?
> What's the main idea, focus, center of gravity here?

2. *Getting Started with Words on Paper.* Here are some suggestions, mostly from Elbow, for getting words down on paper.

> I'm going to write without stopping for exactly ten minutes and find out what happens.
> I'm stuck with this beginning. I've tried three different versions and none of them are right. Never mind, I'll write it through by brute force. If nothing else works, I'll start out with "What I'd like to write about is this_____."
> Whatever I start with will probably be cut out or

revised anyway, so I'll just start in and then go back and fool around with the beginning after I've done the complete draft.

I'm really stuck with this piece. I'm going to pretend that I have a half hour to write out what I'm trying to say to a friend. Here I go.

I'm still stuck. Nothing seems to work. My mind feels like mush, like hot oatmeal. I'd better do something else and then come back fresh. I've had enough experience with this stage to know I'm going nowhere. I'd better leave it and come back to it when I feel better.

3. *Other Advice for Writers During the Drafting Stage.* Don't worry about handwriting, punctuation, spelling, capitalization, format, or paragraphing right now. Just keep on moving. You can always go back. Trust yourself to find out what you want to say. Let your pencil do the talking.

Don't worry about how good it is now. It *will* be good. Trust yourself. What you're writing is important for you.

What you want your students to learn to say to themselves at this frustration stage is something like this:

"I've done a lot of work before the first draft. I've gotten together facts, dates, and specifics, read, talked to some people, made notes, thought about what I want to write about, and have made some kind of scratch outline.

"No more stalling. It's time to begin."

Revising. "Rewriting," says Mario Puzo, as one of his Godfatherly Rules for Writing a Bestselling Novel, "is the whole secret to writing."

Your students must not continue to believe, like all inexperienced writers, that after they finished a first draft and made some minor corrections, that the composing process is over, that they can now "copy it over in ink." But the more they write, the more they know a new kind of work, far different from the spontaneous, intuitive activities of prewriting and drafting, remains. During these first two stages of writing, he or she listened only to self as the writer. Now the writer must think about what the audience will make of the writing and rely on his or her conscious, rational self, and with ruthless calculation, revise the writing so another can read it without obstruction, so there will be no barrier to communication. Donald Hall sums up well the stance a writer must assume at this stage: "The attitude to cultivate from the start is that revision is a way of life." Revision, your students must come to accept, goes with the writer's turf.

Just what is revision? How do we talk about it? Donald Murray describes two kinds of revision. *External revision* -- what I call editing -- has to do with all matters related to proofreading, such as spelling, punctuation, capitalization, and usage. *Internal revision* for Murray, on the other hand, has to do with major changes in a draft, including changes in content--mostly adding specific details or examples--changes in form and structure, changes in language, and even changes in point of view or voice (1978).

Your students need to learn that when they revise, they make more or less conscious decisions about altering significantly what they have written in the first draft. They tinker and reformulate. They rearrange words, trying one word in place of another, possibly replacing it with the original. They tighten up by cutting out unnecessary phrases and clauses. They can change the design of an entire piece by throwing away an extensive opening, moving complete sections around, or substantially revising an ending because the original structure had changed during the writing. They might rewrite the entire piece, changing the tenses of all verbs, switching the point of view, or altering the overall tone of the composition. Or they may even, in some cases, abandon the first draft altogether, at least for the time being, to turn to something else which flows more easily.

After they have produced a first draft, it's necessary that the students get feedback about the piece from somebody who can be viewed as being honest and knowledgeable--what I call a "trusted reader." This can best be done by having the student writers read aloud their drafts in pairs or in small groups of from four to five students. The groups need to be small enough so the writers won't be inhibited by listening to feedback about their writing. The feedback is crucial because it lets the students have an audience, allows them to realize how others perceive their writing. The subject of workshopping and of providing guidelines for the students to follow is a matter of enormous importance. You might, as a start, pursue these writings: Beaven (1956), Blake (1976), Elbow (1973), Macrorie (1980), and Rogers (1961).

Here are some specific activities for you to have your students engage in as they listen to each others' drafts as they read them out aloud in small workshop groups.

Activities for the Revising Stage

1. *Finding Striking Parts.* Elbow calls this "pointing" (pp.85-86). Have students "point out" words or phrases which struck them as beautiful, true, or somehow unusual. Pointing also means noting words or phrases which are especially tried or worn out. Rather than use the pejorative terms "cliché" or "trite"--which is what they are--I call them "easy shots."

What word or phrase stood out most clearly in my mind?

What word or phrase have I heard many times before? "nice guy," "tall, dark, and handsome," "in the nick of time," etc. How can I rephrase it so it's new and fresh?

2. *Finding the Focus.* This is what Elbow calls the "center of gravity." What's the focus?

What dominant impression do I get of this piece? What is the main feeling or most important idea the writer is trying to convey to me?

What one sentence sums up the piece for me?

What one word from the piece summarizes the main idea?

What one word not in the piece summarizes the piece for me?

3. *Determining Structure.* Within this category students ask and answer questions designed to help both readers and writer to see how the piece is put together.

What's the plan of the piece?

How does it fit together?

Can I see the parts clearly?

Do the opening and ending relate to the whole piece? To the focus?

Is there a cyclical or rhythmic pattern to the parts?

4. *Perceiving Unity.* Essentially, here the students

want to relate whether or not the parts relate to the whole.

Have I left out unnecessary or irrelevant stuff? From the whole piece?

From paragraphs or even from sentences?

5. *Achieving Coherence.* With these questions the students try to find whether or not parts lead smoothly one to another.

Have I used devices like repetition of key words or technical devices like transitional words (first, second, therefore, and nevertheless) or have I used key pronouns? Does the writing--sentences as well as paragraphs--proceed smoothly?

6. *Choosing Exact Words.* The traditional term for this category is *diction.* Have I used general words like "nice" and "big" where specific ones are needed?

Have I used big, "schoolish" words where simpler words would be more in keeping with what I'm trying to say?

Have I sometimes used synonyms for a key word?

Or, have I used the same word over again when repetition is called for?

Am I unsure about what words I want to use, or do I know exactly which words go where?

7. *Varied Sentences.* A sign of a mature writer is the ability to use a variety of sentences in his or her writing.

Have I written sentences that are easy and even fun to read?

Have I sometimes combined short, choppy sentences into longer but still readable ones?

Have I, at other times, balanced long, complicated sentences against short and direct sentences?

Have I used my own judgment in revising sentences so they are interesting and occasionally surprising?

8. *Finding the Best Balance Between Specifics and Generalizations.* Effective writers use details and examples to support statements but frame generalizations to give shape to a mass of details. Both specifics and generalizations are important for effective writing.

Have I found enough details to support my thesis?

Does my thesis--implied or stated--support the details I have gathered?

9. *Using Words Related to the Senses.* Words related

to the senses give a rich sense of immediate experience.

Have I used words which make the reader experience the senses of smell, touch, taste, and hearing as well as that of sight?

10. *Showing. Not Telling.* Rather than *telling* that the **person is happy, the experienced writers knows he or she** makes a situation dramatic by *showing* a specific girl as she laughs, claps her hands with delight, and exclaims, "Wow! I feel great!" Have I used details related to the senses, anecdotes, and examples to make my writing vivid, colorful, dramatic, and immediate?

11. *Effective Openers and Satisfying Endings.* Openings and endings are often the most difficult parts of compositions to get just right, and students need to realize these parts never come easily; they must be worked on and worked over before they do the job.

How does the piece open? Does it grab the attention of the reader with an anecdote, a dramatic quotation, or a provocative example?

Does the ending satisfy? Not merely by summarizing what was written before but by leaving the reader with a sense of completeness, with the satisfaction of feeling, "Yes, that's the way this should end."

Editing. Perhaps for experienced writers, there are only three stages to composing in writing: prewriting, drafting, and rewriting and rewriting until one stops. Some writers report they never stop revising until the piece is in print. As one writer commented, "I never stop rewriting, I just let the piece go."

From time to time, your students need to learn how to edit a piece, to prepare it for print. This means that, however distasteful for them, they must observe conventional editing procedures, bringing a paper to as nearly a perfect state as possible. They should learn to be satisfied with nothing less than what editors call "good, clean copy."

The common elements in editing--at least at the simplest level--are these: conventional manuscript format, correct capitalization, spelling, punctuation, and what is traditionally known as acceptable "grammar and usage."

During this editing state--as with all but the drafting

stage--students can help each other. One student can read his or her paper aloud to another, with both of them pointing out errors. Or one student can read to himself or herself a revised manuscript and mark with a pencil all mechanical errors. Several students may take turns editing each others' papers. Or you, as the teacher, can make a quick reading of a students' paper, catching as many mechanical errors as you can. Remember, the more errors you pick up before the last draft, the fewer superficial mistakes you'll be bothered by when you read the final manuscript. As a teacher of writing, your job is not to proofread; that task belongs to the writer.

Here are some simple activities related to the editing stage.

Activities for Editing

1. *Conventional Format.* Have I followed conventional manuscript format? This means I must write on one side only, on 8½ by 11" paper with a pen that does not smudge or blur, or type double-spaced with wide margins all around, on paper which takes writing or typing well (not erasable bond). Have I identified my paper by writing my name, date, title, and the course name--if my teacher wants it--on the first page?

The students should realize that the originality of their papers lies not in the format, mechanics, or in the paper's appearance, but in its content.

2. *Mechanical Errors.* Have I corrected all errors in spelling, punctuation, capitalization, and standard usage?

3. *Proofreading.* Have I made one last reading of my paper to pick up careless errors in handwriting or typing in the final draft?

Teach students to listen to their inner speech and to put down what they hear on paper. Teach them to follow the composing process, for composing *is* the curriculum. It is a model for seeing, thinking, perceiving, writing, and interacting with other human beings. Writing through composing is a model which actually defines us as human beings.

THE INSTRUCTIONAL COMPOSING PROCESS

Model for Creating Writing Lessons

Type of Writing _____

Title of Writing Activity _____

_____

Grade Level _____ Teacher _____

The Instructional Composing Process Format

General Approach		Specific Application
	1. Stimulus	--an idea to which students may react; may be in the form of a film, picture, reading, discussion, or experience.
PREWRITING		
	2. Prewriting	--opportunity for students to explore the stimulus; may be discussion, research, study guide. Should focus on specific areas (e.g. conflict, character, setting, etc.) preparatory to writing.
DRAFTING		
	3. First (rough) draft	--concerned with getting thoughts on paper, not with revising or editing.
	4. Skills Instruction (optional)	--work on one or two specific skills, e.g., workshopping, end marks, agreement, commas. Use students' own works as much as possible. Allows students to apply skills instruction immediately.
REVISING		
	5. Revising/Workshopping	--opportunity for students to examine their writing and share ideas with others before writing the final draft. Often works best moving from pairs to small groups to whole class. Concentration should be on total discourse and specific skills to be developed.
EDITING		
	6. Second (Final)	--incorporate suggestions from workshopping and concepts from skills instruction.
	7. Submission	--for reaction, not grade. Unless the student has not revised or incorporated skills instruction in this draft, the student should not rewrite it.

Bibliography

Beaven, Mary. "Individualized Goal Setting, Self Evaluation, and Peer Evaluation," *Evaluating Writing*. Urbana, Illinois: NCTE, 1977, pp. 135-156.

Blake, Robert W. and Frederick B. Tuttle, Jr. *Composing As The Curriculum: A Guide for Instruction in Written Composition, Grades K-12*. Albion, NY: Albion Public Schools, 1978.

.... "Writing for the Left Hand: Writing Activities for the Intermediate Grades," *Facilitating Language Development*. Buffalo, NY: State University of New York at Buffalo, 1978.

.... "How to Talk to a Writer, or Forward to Fundamentals in Teaching Writing," *English Journal*, Vol. 65 (November, 1976), No. 8: 49-55.

Bradbury, Ray. "How to Keep and Feed a Muse." *On Writing, By Writers*, ed. William West. Boston: Ginn and Company, 1966.

Didion, Joan. "Why I Write," *The New York Times Book Review*, December 5, 1976, p. 98.

Elbow, Peter. *Writing Without Teachers*. New York: Oxford University Press, 1973.

Emig, Janet. "Hand, Eye, Brain: Some 'Basics' in Writing Processs," *Research on Composing*, ed. Charles R. Cooper and Lee Odell. Urbana, IL: NCTE, 1978.

.... "Writing as a Mode of Learning," *College Composition and Communication*, May, 1977.

.... *The Composing Processes of Twelfth Graders*. Urbana, IL: NCTE, 1978.

.... "The Uses of the Unconscious in Composing," *College Composition and Communication*, XV (February, 1964), 1.

Koch, Kenneth. *Wishes, Lies, and Dreams: Teaching Children to Write Poetry*. New York: Vintage Books, 1970.

Lopate, Phillip. "Helping Young Children Start to Write," *Research on Composing*. Urbana, IL: NCTE, 1978, pp. 135-149.

Macrorie, Ken. "The Helping Circle," *Telling Writing*. Rochelle Park, NJ: Hayden Book Company, Inc., 1980.

Mills, Hilary, "Creators on Creating: William Styron," *Saturday Review*, (September 1980), pp. 46-50.

Moffett, James. "Integrity in the Teaching of Writing," *Phi Delta Kappan,* Vol. 61 (December, 1979), No. 4: 276-279.

Murray, Donald M. "Internal Revision: A Process of Discovery," *Research on Composing,* ed. Charles R. Cooper and Lee Odell. Urbana, IL: NCTE, 1978.

Ornstein, Robert E. *The Psychology of Consciousness.* New York: Penguin Books, Inc., 1972.

Rogers, Carl. "The Characteristics of a Helping Relationship," *On Becoming a Person.* Boston: Houghton Mifflin Company, 1961.

Stafford, William. "A Way of Writing," *Responding: Three,* ed. Robert Weinberger and Nathan S. Blount. Lexington, MA: Ginn and Company, 1973, pp. 44-46.

Vonnegut, Kurt. "How to Write with Style," Advertisement for International Paper Company, Elmsford, NY, 1980.

Welty, Eudora. "Review of Selected Letters of William Faulkner, *The New York Times Book Review.* February 6, 1977, p. 30.

TEACHING WRITING SKILLS THROUGH PEER EVALUATION

Jerome F. Megna
Brooklyn College

English teachers often experience boredom and frustration during the endless hours they spend correcting students' themes. Students' reactions to corrected themes often reinforce English teachers' deepest feelings of abject futility. It was during the depths of my own abysmal desperation over lack of student improvement in writing that there occurred to me a method of teaching composition, having students write willingly, and evaluating the writing, without having to spend entire weekends grading themes. The method, S.E.G., is an acronym for the three phases of the program: sensitivity exposure, and grading. S.E.G. can operate intensively throughout an entire semester or can be used two periods a week.

The method is based on a peer group system of evaluation which encourages total student participation, democratic decision-making, periodic assessment of criteria, and self-evaluation. The emphasis in the program is on writing for an audience, peers who provide individual as well as collaborative feedback. The three phases of the S.E.G. method are predicated on the following assumptions:

1. many students feel embarrassed or inhibited in writing what they feel, what they believe, and what they experience;
2. the learning environment is positively affected by a mutual sharing of values, interests, backgrounds, and experiences;
3. working in small, cohesive groups facilitates learning and encourages self-confidence;
4. a teacher's shared participation in the learning process fosters student initiative and motivation;
5. criteria for evaluation best come from students themselves;
6. students do well to become actively involved in the process of reading critically each other's writing as well as in doing their own writing;

7. improvement in writing ability comes in graduated and successive stages;
8. publicly agreed to standards, immediate and honest feedback, and a chance to defend one's position all contribute to an atmosphere of intellectual growth necessary to raise the level of writing performance;
9. the more practice one gets in writing, the better writer one becomes; and
10. recognition of how one's theme ranks in relation to four or five others does not necessarily have a debilitating effect upon a student's desire to improve, but rather may encourage him or her to explore other alternatives the next time he or she writes for an audience. Two absolute conditions for success in the program are a class's willingness to improve its writing skills and a teacher's sensitive responsiveness to students who need help on an individual level.

The first phase of the program, "sensitivity," involves creating an atmosphere of trust and confidence so that the students and the teacher may be willing to express their personal feelings without defensiveness and to accept the feeling of others without hostility. Techniques for the achievement of these goals will vary, depending upon class size, existing conditions of class intimacy, and general level of maturity. Activities contained in Sidney B. Simon's *Values Clarification* or Gay Henricks' *The Centering Book,* both in paperback, have proved helpful in establishing such a climate of trust and confidence.

One technique I have found useful is the conducting of a group interview. For students unsure of interview methods, I call on a volunteer to come to the front of the room, sit at the teacher's desk, and respond to my interview questions which I ask from the back of the room. He or she can "pass" on any question I ask. At the end of the interview, I ask the rest of the class to rate my questions as to their effectiveness in eliciting from the interviewed student information which helped us understand him or her better and which permitted us to grow closer to him or her on a personal level. Instead of asking the class to rank specific questions, it is sometimes more valuable to ask them at a later session which questions they remembered as being the most useful because of the information they triggered from the respondent. During the interview, students should be asking themselves: What makes a "valuable" question? What kinds of questions reveal a person's character? When should follow-up questions on the related topic be pursued? All students should be encouraged to jot down the questions they find useful.

Samples of questions during this session may include the following:
1. How old are you? Do you like being that age? Why or why not?
2. If you had your preference, what age would you like to be? Why?
3. Do you think age makes a big difference in how people relate to one another? In what way -- if any?
4. Does it ever happen that older (or younger) people make you nervous? In what way -- if any?
5. Do older (or younger) people ever get in your way? How? -- if they do.
6. Are most of your friends older or younger than you? Why is this so?
7. Do you think that parents can ever be friends? When?
8. What are some things that most annoy you about certain friends?
9. When are you the most talkative? Why?
10. What kind of people make you feel the most comfortable? Why?
11. What do you do to relax?
12. Do you have any special projects which you like working on?
13. If you had your wish, what important thing would you like to do in your life?
14. Which characteristics of a friend's personality do you like least? Which do you like best?
15. If you could change one thing about a friend's personality, what would it be?

16. In what ways are you different from most of your friends?

Naturally, each of these questions can be followed up with other questions which relate specifically to the theme around which the question is based. For example:

Q: What do you do to relax?
A: I play the guitar.
Q: How often do you play it?
A: Nearly every day.
Q: For how long?
A: Sometimes an hour or so.
Q: Does anyone listen to you?
A: No, I'm always alone.
Q: What kind of songs do you play?
A: Anything that comes into my head. Sometimes it's what I just heard on the radio. Other times I make up my own tune.
Q: Do you have a favorite kind of music? etc. . . .

After a few group interviews, students should be prepared to conduct them individually with one another. Ask them to take notes on a series of interviews limited to five minutes for each interview. The time, of course, is arbitrary and may be extended. After they interview the subject, the subject has the opportunity to interview them. The teacher should signal four five-minute interview segments and, at the end of twenty minutes, ask selected members of the class to give a profile of someone they interviewed -- based on the notes they took. Then ask the class to judge how well the details selected for the profile reveal the dimensions of a classmate's personality. Initially it might be advisable to keep the profiles anonymous. As the class comes to know one another more intimately, however, the identify of the profile could be shared without embarrassment. In my experience, it has helped enormously for me to have involved myself in this activity in the same manner the students do. This creates the climate of shared participation and mutual trust. Bonds are formed; experiences are exchanged; and group feelings are consolidated. This initial phase may last for two weeks.

There are, of course, many variations and possibilities to the "sensitivity" aspect of the S.E.G. program.

However, the goals of this phase may be broadly summarized as follows:
1 - to break down barriers of inhibition and mistrust;
2 - to provide opportunities for establishing friendships;
3 - to encourage maximum participation; and
4. - to enable students to come to know one another sufficiently so that they may later establish cohesive groups of four or five.

In a word, "sensitivity" aims at establishing a positive classroom atmosphere through exercises which foster affective learning. As the program progresses, I have found it useful to return to the "sensitivity" phase periodically to permit emotional feedback or dissipate occasional hostilities, to reaffirm group consciousness, or simply to refine aspects of the program.

The formation of workable groups should be one of the more concrete and obvious results of this first phase. Ideally, the natural evolution of a group of four or five students will emerge as the exercises make close group work necessary. For example, the teacher may ask that groups of four or five be formed arbitrarily and that each group decide consensually how to respond to the following tasks:

Task 1 - A middle-aged woman, with no immediate relatives, informs that she has 24 hours to live. She wants you to be "program directors" for her and plan her day. She will bequeath to the entire group her sizable fortune if the group's plan is acceptable to her. She agrees to answer only ten questions before the group formulates its plan. What ten questions do you absolutely need answered before you can begin the planning? Decide as a group what you would plan for her last 24 hours. (The teacher may play the role of the woman and supply the answers to the group's ten questions.)

Task 2 - Create a group abstract drawing or doodle and write, as a group, either an interpretation of its meaning or a poem which "fits" its meaning.

Task 3 - Write a complete description of the ugliest mortal ever to have existed.

Task 4 - Write fifteen half-complete "if" sentences which, when completed by an individual, will give you a good clue to what that person is like. For example, "If I could guarantee the enforcement of three laws, they would be. . . ."

Task 5 - Complete the "if" statements of another group in such a way as to create a very unusual character.

Task 6 - Make up a fifteen line nonsense poem that rhymes.

Examples can grow increasingly complete as the group's interation improves. Before final consolidation of groups, students may be encouraged to trade membership with another group -- so long as they find a willing classmate. Critical, however, to group work is that the problem or task be well defined, that the group's solution be made public as soon as possible, and that there be feedback to the solution. If groups have difficulty forming, the teacher may hasten the process. Groups can be built around similarities of interest, attitudes, or values. On the other hand, they can be initially formed on the basis of such inconsequential criteria as dissimilarities of neighborhood, sibling composition, or even birth month. Ideally, the group should be heterogeneous; for this reason the teacher may wish to intrude in the process of group formation.

After experimenting with several different group constructs, students may have special preferences for the group to which they wish to belong. If a particular groups "jells" after several sessions it is best to keep it together. One of the final goals of the sensitivity phase is to establish group cohesion. If that cohesion comes early in the process, so much the better. In any case, after the groups form, the teacher should devise strategies which establish solidarty within the group.

Teachers who have used the S.E.G. approach to writing have suggested the following strategies:
1. If there is a photographer in the class, let him or her take a picture of each group. But the group must first decide how they will pose, what the background for the photograph will be, etc. The pictures should hang in the room with an approprite blurb under them.
2. Let the group decide upon a group name, a five-

digit number code, and a secret word which only they know. Suggest that the name, number, and word be based on a rearrangement of the letters of their names and the months or days of their birth.
3. Ask the group to write five adjectives which aptly reflect a positive characteristic of each member in the group.
4. Ask the group to decide on a list of five favorite things or people in which they are in unanimous agreement. Possible "favorites" might include a food, a ball player, a make of car, a movie star, a song, an occupation, etc.

Techniques in establishing solidarity among groups can be multiplied. It is better to space such activities at intervals throughout the term rather than have them occur repeatedly within a short period of time.

The second phase, "exposure," may take from four to seven separate sessions, but this may vary from class to class. Like "sensitivity," it should reoccur periodically. "Exposure" entails showing students the process of how themes are corrected and evaluated. Here, the teacher has the opportunity to "think out loud" as he or she corrects individual themes on an overhead projector. To initiate this phase, the entire class is asked to write in pencil a paragraph or two on any subject of their choosing. After making transparencies of fifteen or twenty of the compositions, the teacher begins the evaluation process on an overhead projector. It is best to preserve the anonymity of each sample of writing. A magic marker or grease pencil is useful for corrections and marginalia. After the first few sessions, students may wish to suggest the codification of uniform correction symbols and uniform grading practices. Or, the students may decide that the assigning of a grade is not appropriate at all.

The critical aspect of "exposure" is to have students determine useful criteria in evaluating a theme and constructive reactions in response to it. In a word, a reader must provide sensitive and appropriate feedback, if a writer is to grow. Students will ordinarily not be able to develop useful criteria at the outset of the "exposure" phase; after they observe how the teacher's process of theme grading occurs, they may decide to reject applying what they consider the teacher's standards. It is important that the teacher be both patient and flexible with the class at this phase. Initially many classes want only "level of interest" to be the criterion used in theme evaluation; other classes have added to this that themes be free of mechanical errors such as misspelling, incorrect punctuation, or gross grammatical errors; still other classes have requested that more sophisticated criteria be included: sentence pattern variation, stylistic consistency, accurate diction, syntactic balance, etc. So long as students have the opportunity to amend their initial criteria, progress will occur.

After being exposed to a teacher's method of correcting themes, a useful exercise is to ask students to evaluate the various observations made on the paper. For example, they could be asked to respond to the following observations:
1. I thought this was boring;
2. I had difficulty following your thinking;
3. To me, it seemed that you jumped from subject to subject without giving me any reason why. For example, on page two of your theme....

Students are quick to see the uselessness of abstract, negative comments and the benefit of concrete ones. A student once suggested that all personal comments begin with "to me, it seemed that...." The class unanimously agreed with this "diplomatic," general-semantic approach to observations, but later decided to refine their position when several students got back on peer evaluations "To me, it seemed that your whole theme stunk."

Constructive reactions, however, pose less of a challenge than useful criteria -- although the two are closely related. An approach for getting students to determine criteria is to ask them, after they have read a fellow-student's theme from the overhead projector, what questions should a reader ask himself/herself to find out how good a piece of writing this is. An alternate method would be for the teacher to present a list of possible questions for the class to rate a writing standards. Such a list might include the following questions:

1. Does this theme have a purpose?
2. What is the point of this paragraph?
3. Was the point developed or was there jumping around from one thing to another without connection?
4. Does this sentence show a clear relationship to the previous one(s)?
5. Does this paragraph have some relationship with the previous one(s)?
6. Is the material arranged in such a manner as to make me curious, to make me want to continue reading?
7. Does the writing, spelling, or grammar interfere with a smooth reading?
8. Does this sentence leave me feeling that I'm not quite sure what the writer meant?
9. Are my opinions affected in any way by this theme?
10. If the author makes a generalization or forms an opinion, does he back up what he says?
11. Are there sufficient details provided?
12. Are there too many useless details provided?
13. Does the writer use words in a fresh, creative, and interesting manner?
14. Are there many phrases which are overused and trite?
15. Do the sentences reflect clarity of thought and precision of meaning?
16. What is my personal reaction to this writing? Do I feel disgust, pain, empathy, fascination, etc.?

Students can easily generate many more pertinent questions. Teachers may be surprised to discover, however, what students rate as the more important criteria in evaluating a theme. Students can more easily internalize and accept standards which they are responsible for developing. Standards which may appear too trival or to subjective to the teacher may have great meaning for the students initially; they should be left to discover for themselves the relative merit of the choices they make.

As the sessions progress and more students express themselves on the evaluation process, the class as a whole will begin to evolve its own philosophy of evaluation through establishing guidelines for the writing of themes. The phase is both dialectic and democratic in that students make suggestions regarding grading procedure and decide consensually on the value of that procedure. The students should be told that they will eventually assume the responsibility of applying these criteria to one another's themes. When all the students understand and agree to the method of evaluation, the second phase of the program is completed. As indicated earlier, sessions in "exposure" should reoccur throughout the term in order to permit students to reevaluate and adjust their standards.

"Grading" is the final and most complex phase of the program. Before beginning this phase, students ought to be in established groups of from four to six. If the tasks assigned during the "sensitivity" phase have not caused all the groups to be formed, a teacher's intervention may be necessary at this time. By the "grading" phase, each group should have the following characteristics:
1. strong rapport,
2. evident solidarity,
3. a willingness and ability to work together on solutions to problems, and
4. an abilty to apply agreed upon criteria to a theme.

The problem of the "grading" phase will be for the group to rank the papers they read according to the criteria the class has established. At the beginning of this session, a secretary for each group should be elected. It is the secretaries' responsibility to facilitate the procedure for the grading sessions. After the election of secretaries, the teacher assigns the first theme to the entire class. It is suggested that the first theme be from three to four hundred words in length and stapled in the upper left-hand corner. The first page of each theme should be the title page and this should contain only the following information:
1. the last four digits of the social security or phone number of the student;
2. the title and date of the theme; and
3. the chronological number of the theme which the student is writing.

The grading session begins by having the secretaries of each group collect the themes from each student in their respective groups. After they check to see that the themes are nameless and numbered, they should give their batch of themes to the secretary of a designated row. If there are four groups, the first theme grading session can be arranged as follows:
> Group 1 will give their themes to Group 2
> Group 2 will give their themes to Group 3
> Group 3 will give their themes to Group 4
> Group 4 will give their themes to Group 1

In order not to penalize any group by having their papers stiffly graded by the same group consecutively, the numerical pattern should be shifted during the next grading session:
> Group 1 will give their themes to Group 4
> Group 2 will give their themes to Group 1
> Group 3 will give their themes to Group 2
> Group 4 will give their themes to Group 3

During the third grading sessions, another combination of groups should be arranged. The teacher should record the shifting patterns of exchange so that no one group receives the same batch of papers for two consecutive sessions.

Besides theme collection and distribution, the secretary of each groups has three specific resonsibilities:
1. to make sure each person in his or her group has the opportunity to read, comment upon and provide evaluation feedback on each theme;
2. to inscribe in Roman numbers in the upper left hand corner of each title page the "rank" to which the group has collectively assigned it; and
3. to staple quarter sheets of paper (q-sheets) to the top middle portion of the title page of each theme.

The Roman number rank is based upon what the group as a whole decides which of the themes is the best, the second best, and so forth. They may decide this by secret vote or by averaging the theme's "position" on an arbitrary scale which the group has agreed to. The criteria for the best theme may be creativity, originality, interest, or anything else which the class had collectively decided during the "exposure" session that an outstanding theme should possess. Themes receiving the number one rank from each group should be dittoed and distributed to the entire class for discussion during a future "exposure" session. These themes and the ensuing class discussion of them will provide the basis for an evaluation and adjustment of standards.

Before beginning to evaluate the themes, each person in a group should have as many q-sheets as there are themes for his or her group to grade. Each q-sheet should contain the following information:
1. the last four digits of the social security or phone number of the theme which is being graded;
2. the personal, subjective comments which the grader wishes to make;
3. a grade or relative position on an arbitrary scale the class had previously agreed to; for example 15/20 could mean 15 points out of a possible 20; and
4. the full signature of the grader.

Using the symbols agreed to in phase two of the program, students should correct the mechanical errors on the theme itself. These are usually mistakes in spelling, diction, punctuation, grammar, or organization and logic. If an evaluator is unsure of the mechanical correctness of a theme he or she is grading, he or she is encouraged to ask the fellow members of his or her group or the teacher for assistance. His or her more personal reactions are written on the q-sheet. These reactions provide the basis for constructive feedback and may include the responses to the questions raised during the "exposure" phase. After evaluating a theme and writing a q-sheet for it, the evaluator should pass only the theme along to the next person in his or her group. The evaluator should hold on to the q-sheet. In this way students are not affected by the evaluations and reactions to the theme by a previous reader. By and large, students view this aspect of the program very seriously and come to have great respect for the compexity and merit of an honest evaluation process.

When all the students of one group have read and graded all the themes assigned to them, they may assist the secretary in stapling or paper-clipping all the q-sheets from every member of the group to the top middle portion of each of the respective title pages. Each theme, then, will have as many q-sheets attached to it as there are readers in the group. It is at this point that the secretary attempts to elicit from his or her group the theme they consider the best, the second best, etc. He or she then inscribes this "rank" in Roman numbers in the upper left-hand corner of the title page. When the best theme from each group is dittoed, distributed, and discussed, the teacher should prod the class into adjusting its standards for future "grading" sessions. The later distribution of the best themes provides an incentive for all students to write an especially good theme for the next "grading" session.

When the themes are returned to the students who wrote them, they reread their themes with the corrections, comments and evaluations. They then write their own evaluation at the end of the theme. The evaluations they received on the q-sheets may not always correlate and it may happen that a student feels that some of the comments made about his or her theme are unfair or irrelevant. He or she should be encouraged to discuss with the readers why they gave the evaluation they did. The writer should include the outcome of such discussion in the self-evaluation. Beneath his or her own reactions to the comments and his or her evaluation of the merit of the corrections and evaluations received from the group, the student then assigns himself or herself a grade. This grade may correspond to the mean or median grade assigned by the groups who corrected the theme, but this should be determined by the individual student. At the very end of the "grading" session, the teacher collects all themes. By reading the comments and evaluations of the group who evaluated each paper, their corrections and marginalia on the theme, and the reaction, defense (if any), and self-evaluation of the student who wrote the theme, the teacher can diagnose the difficulties of the writer in a fraction of the time it would take to grade the paper traditionally.

By the third theme grading session, the elaborate procedures of the S.E.G. method are carried out effortlessly by the students. Significant improvement in writing techniques and style will be apparent to anyone who reads themes from the first grading session and then reads them from the fourth or fifth session. Students, given their choice, almost always prefer the active, self-evaluating S.E.G. method to the more traditional methods of learning principles of writing expository prose, applying those principles in a theme, and having that theme corrected and graded by a teacher who may have 100 to 200 such themes to mark and record before returning them. Moreover, there will be greater opportunity to assign themes more frequently, feedback on the themes will be almost immediate, and teachers will be able to spend more time conferring with individual students who need special help. While no single approach to teaching compostion can guarantee success in every instance, the S.E.G. approach engages students in the proceses of writing, reading, and evaluating themes in a most direct manner. The method encourages purposefulness in writing, sensitivity in reading, and responsibility in evaluating

II. PRODUCT

THE YOUNG STUDENT WRITERS
Charles R. Chew
Bureau of English and Reading Education

Can the young student write? How much? How often? How well? and What? are questions asked as attention focuses on instruction in written composition. The material which follow attempts to answer some of these questions through a limited examination of one writing program and a sample of student writing. In this discussion, more questions may be raised than answered.

The writer produces the written piece and both the writer and the written piece are important as the educator and researcher try to gain knowledge about the skills of written composition and how they are developed. Recent research amplifies the concept that the production of written composition requires a process; and in the process, the writer and the product must be carefully scrutinized to make determinations relative to instruction.

Much evidence now exists from the work of Donald Graves and researchers working with him at the University of New Hampshire to convince us that young children can indeed write if given the opportunity to do so. Enough evidence also exists to suggest that students at the end of their school experience (Grade 12) have not developed their skill to the potential suggested in the early grades as documented by Graves' research.

A legitimate question to ask is whether children in the "normal" school classroom, uninspired by the researcher, can likewise write. I believe that we already have evidence to answer with an unqualified "yes" and more data accumulate each day. The observation discussed below serves as an illustration.

I recently had an opportunity to observe a first grade class in a Brooklyn public school. I spent a whole day with the class in as unobtrusive a way as possible -- observing classroom instruction and environment, talking with teachers and students, and listening to the sounds and conversations around me.

The class, I was told, is typical of the school. According to the teacher, the students are a little below average academically. All students come from a "blue collar," ethnic home. No parent would be considered a professional. At least three students spoke no English when they entered the class in September, and three students were repeaters. The point that I am trying to make is that this class is not an academically select one but rather a very typical type of class.

The teacher asked the children at the beginning of my visit why they had a visitor. The hands shot into the air, and the response was that I had come to watch them write. The teacher followed this response with another question which wondered why anyone would want to do that. The class responded, "Because we are all authors and illustrators," and that response set the tone for my day's observation.

Each student in this first grade does indeed consider herself or himself to be an author and illustrator. To support this idea, all students have writing folders in which whole pieces of writing are kept. Each student has also written one book (in most cases more) in addition to the work found in the folder.

Writing in this first grade is an integral part of every experience that the student has in class. Writing is used as a lead into the reading lesson or follows directly from it. When the community, classroom jobs, science experiments, and holidays are the focal point for classroom discussion and interest, writing is a natural part of that experience. Writing also springs from students' interests and personal activities. (See Example #1).

Each student has a buddy who listens to what has been written or reads it. The buddy makes positive comments about the written piece and also raises pertinent questions. This activity is reinforced through the practice of having several students each day read something he or she has written. The individual or class listens and responds to these types of questions. What is the piece about? What did I like about this piece? Does it make sense? What don't I understand? The author, after this, work needs to be done, if any.

In such a practice, students develop their listening skills and their ability to summarize. They develop the skill -- if even in its infancy -- to recognize strengths and

EXAMPLE #1

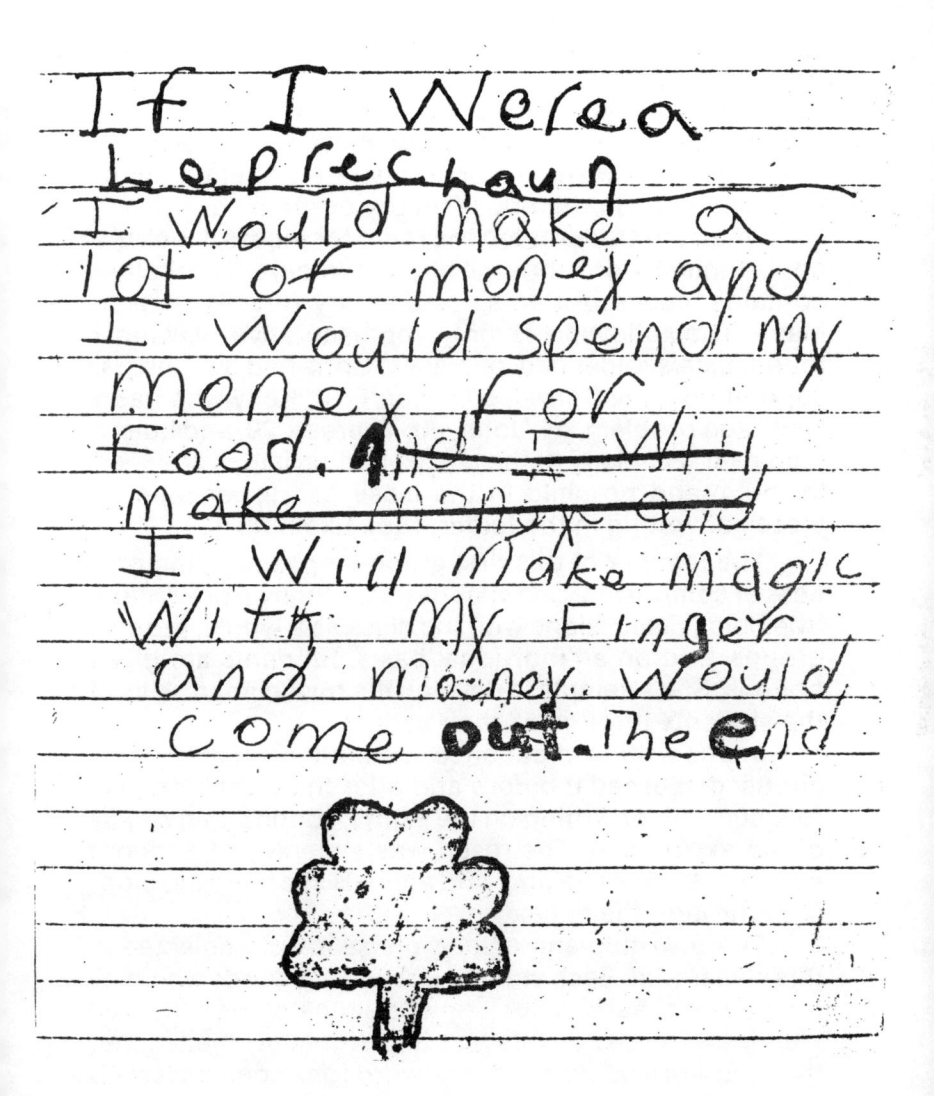

If I were a Leprechaun
I would make a lot of money and I would spend my money for food. And I will make money and I will make magic with my finger and money would come out. The end

weaknesses of a written piece. In addition, they learn to be supportive of another's effort, to become acquainted with the ideas of others, and to share in the knowledge of the writer.

The teacher of this first grade is a gifted teacher, of that I am convinced, but gifted in the sense that she brings to her classroom enthusiasm, an awe of children, a willingness to try something different, and a desire to develop students' abilities to an optimum. She is not gifted in the sense that she knows all the recent research in written composition nor has she an abundance of college credits in rhetoric -- theory or practice.

When the students left the room for recess, I took the opportunity to look through student folders. Each folder contains pieces written since January (my visit was in May). The following is only representative of what I found. Lisa's folder had 38 pieces; Chris had 30; Christa, 85; Anthony, 28; Darrell, 50; Cheryl, 16; Kelly who has a language problem, 64; John, 40; Theresa, 29; and Luis, a hold over, 25. Many of the pieces had revisions attached to them, and no child in the class had fewer than 16 pieces of writing in the folder. (See Example #2.)

The teacher of this first grade emphasizes the process of composing. She spends much time on prewriting. She holds discussions with the class as a whole, in small groups, and on an individual basis. Students are given options. She attempts to develop the observation skills of the students through all their senses.

In one writing experience, the students had visited a circus, discussed it before and after the visit; then they focused in their writing on the sights, sounds, and smells of the experience. The result was a medley of popcorn popping, barkers yelling, and animals snarling and clopping through their acts.

The rewriting and editing phase is not neglected in this classroom. Each student knows that words which he or she is not sure of spelling should be circled thereby cluing the reader to this fact and signaling the teacher that this word could become a word for a spelling lesson or an entry in an individual's spelling book.

Each student has a check sheet to use with his or her own piece and with the buddy's piece. Briefly, the sheet includes the following.

EXAMLE #2

John M.   January 14 1981
Class   1-125

All About Dinosaurs

Millions of years ago dinosaurs walked on earth. Some were meat eaters and others were plant eaters. These are names of dinosaurs Tyrannosaurus, Triceratops, Brontosaurus, Allosaurs, Diplodoc Mammoth and Stegosaurus. I like dinosaurs because they're cute.

Check Sheet
Name _____
   I can use
     Periods _____   Question Marks _____
     Capitals_____   Quotation Marks _____
   My story
    1. Makes sense_____
    2. Has whole sentences_____
    3. Has a
       beginning
       middle
       end
    4. Stays on the topic

Those who question the place of writing in the first grade, may ask what has been neglected in the program. In this particular classroom, the answer would be nothing. The students have learned all their sight words. They have covered the expected lessons in reading. They have had their phonics drill. They have been through their spellers. In addition, the teacher is convinced, and so are the parents, that the students have gained a great deal.

Through writing, these students have integrated many of the language skills that are often kept discrete. Comprehension has taken on a new meaning because their reading of each other's writing has the dimension of personal communication. Reading and writing have become functional as communication. Each student's self-esteem has been positively reinforced because each student has proved to be an author and illustrator.

I personally believe that observation of the writer involved in the writing process will further develop our understanding of and knowledge about written composition. However, we do not always have the opportunity to observe students at different grade levels on a day-to-day basis as they struggle as writers. We must many times turn to the product--the piece that the student has written. There is much to learn from this experience as well. The students' papers can and do tell us a great deal. We may need to refocus our questions as we examine these written pieces in a way to discover what it is that students can do.

We have recently read approximately 800 papers written by students in grades 2-5. Papers in this sample were written by students in a specific school district in the state. The district is a typical small city type with students of multi-ethnic backgrounds. The writing tasks were given to the students in a near testlike situation (perhaps not the most conducive way to inspire good writing), and we do not really know how much experience the students had as writers.

We found in the better papers of Grade 2 students that the students entered into the experience in the writing, handled time sequences, used "if I were ... I would" "because," "then," "next," and used adjectives. At times, there was a playfulness with the language.

In reading papers written by second grade students, we found that these students could generate a number of words on one topic. They could relate a number of ideas to the same topic although initially they simply listed the ideas in a series and some compositions lack an internal coherence; however, the papers written later in the school year by second graders showed that these students could give a number of details to support one idea, and unity and coherence became more evident. The second grader can enter the writing through his or her own experience, can handle time sequence, reporting, and conditional tense. The writer can use repetition effectively and can use adjectives to enhance description. The second grader knows how to punctuate with end punctuation, spell surprisingly well, and use capital letters at the beginning of sentences.

Shannon in Grade 2 wrote

If I were a Monkey
If I were a Monkey
I would climb trees, and I would jump from branch to branch all day long. I would have lots of monkey friends to play with. I would live in the zoo or the jungle and I would get out of my cage. I would look out of my cage. And I would love being a monkey.

In looking at the papers written by third grade students, the reader becomes aware that children can write more. They can attend to the task and expand it. The second grade student seems willing to stay with a topic such as "My favorite animal is ..." In the third grade, children are not only willing to write about animals but sports, people, and teams as well. The good writer can amplify the topic and use facts to embellish it. The better writers seem to have a knowledge of the world and are eager to share this knowledge through their writing (O.J. Simpson's record, world series standings).

The handling of the conventions of language (spelling, punctuation, capitalization, and word choice) becomes more sophisticated. The third grade student can use a direct quotation which suggests that the writer can conceptualize the role of a person in a story. (This skill was used by first grade students discussed earlier in this article). The third grade writer can use the appositive, the introductory subordinate clause, connectors other than "and," and parentheses.

Andrew in Grade 3 wrote

If I had a Balloon

If I had a balloon, I would sail over houses and tree tops. I would fly higher then some airplanes. I would race some boats across the Hudson River. I would make some floats so I could land on water. (Even though it was a balloon.) If I had a balloon, I would land on the Tappan Zee Bridge. (If I had special landing gear.) And I would fly off and do many wonderous things if I had a balloon.

I wish someday I will get a balloon.

As we read papers written by fourth grade students, we saw the continued development of a number of the skills already noted for earlier grade students.

The fourth grade writer can show the relationships of characters, develops a story line, projects himself into the experience, makes extended associations, continues to employ repetition, demonstrates an understanding of and the interplay between fantasy and reality. The writer has the ability to relate events to nature, to extend the composition structure, to list, to classify and to contrast. The writer can begin with a generalization and move to specifics, using in some cases ten to fifteen specifics. As the writer works, she or he imposes an organizational pattern on the written piece and prioritizes the details given.

Thor in Grade 4 wrote

My Special Place

My special place is a room. A very small room, in fact. It is behind my elevator in the house. To get in, I have to squeeze by a metal shaft. Then I can do anything I want.

Before we moved in, the room led under the front stairs and stopped at a window. Back then it was used to store things in.

When we moved in, and I was born, my brother Erik and Cris and my sisters Sigrid and Sonja played house in the room. Sometimes they used me as the baby.

Now I'm the only one who can get into the room. I have covered it with tar, a peephole, a shelf and table, and me. Sometimes I play Secret Spy 107-AZ.

The skills evidenced in the papers read from the earlier grades are also found in the papers from grade five, and it would serve no purpose to repeat all of them. With better writers, handwriting, spacing, and the use of margins seem to be entirely under control. The writer experiments with style and figurative language. The writer can now impose his other knowledge of a literary form on the composition by recording and inter-relating personal experience with the literary experience. The writer incorporates the elements of time, mood, and setting into the piece. The better writer is now able to accomplish the assigned task by producing a very tightly structured piece of writing. Such a writer also shows a broader understanding of word choice and word associations. (See Examples #3 and #4.)

The preceding discussion fully recognizes that not all students at these various grade levels produce writing equally well or of the same quality. The discussion attempts to focus on what students *can* do, and the time may be right to focus on the positive rather than the negative. If nothing emerges from the discussion of the class observation and the deductions from reading student papers other than the fact that young children *can* write, a beginning has been made. Of course, much more remains to be done.

EXAMPLE #3

Just last month I was picked for a character in the play "Oliver." When I went to tryouts the first time I had the jitters, and the next day I got called back to tryouts and I had made it! I had the part, the Artful Dodger. At the first couple of pratices I was terrible. One day I had to stay after school for some extra pratice. In the last two weeks I have improved considerably. Infact the director of the play says, I may steal the show.

EXAMPLE #4

When I was almost five years old I had older brothers and sisters. I was the middle sister of the family. My older brothers and sisters got what they wanted now and then because they were older, and my younger brother and sisters got what they wanted most of the time because they were younger. I had felt quite left out and could not hold back my tears sometimes. It felt as though nobody loved me, and it didn't seem fair that my Mom and Dad gave the other kids favors and other nice things like that.

As I grew older my mind understood a bit more, and I acted a bit more mature than I did before. I began to notice that I had been loved all this time, and had shed many tears for nothing. Indeed many years had passed by fast and all my ways and actions with them. I finally thought to myself, I was really growing up, yes really growing up!

Systematic observations of students involved in the writing process at all grade levels must be completed. A more extensive reading of student papers becomes a necessity. Questions must be raised about types of topics, time on task, and instructional strategies.

I suggest that this work begin in earnest now.

STUDENTS COMPOSE: WRITER'S WORKSHOP*

Sheila A. Schlawin and Charles R. Chew
New York State Education Department

Can what we know about how children compose be translated into practical classroom application to help children develop writing skills? Do you really know much about children's composing process?

A challenge to deal with these questions came to us in the form of an invitation to conduct a Writers' Workshop for fourth, fifth, and sixth grade children in a nearby elementary school. The workshop was to be for all the children in those grades, not just the ones who were considered by their teachers to be superior writers. The teahers were to participate in the workshop, as it was meant to be a learning experience for the teachers as well as the children.

Our first step was to meet with the teachers to discuss what the objective for each grade would be. The teachers selected an objective from their language arts syllabus for each grade. For the fourth grade it was to relate an event in chronological order, for the fifth, to write a composition using cause and effect, and for the sixth, to write a paragraph with a topic sentence and supporting detail.

Our next step was to consider what we know about how children compose. Perhaps it would be better to say what we *infer* from various studies rather than what we *know*, definitively.

First, we infer from Loban's extensive longitudinal study of language development, that although oral and written language are somewhat different, the development of written language is to a large extent dependent on oral (Loban, 1976). The work of Lundsteen (1976) and others demonstrates that oral activities stimulate the process of composing as children not only speak, but think and experience.

Over the years, a definitive number of studies indicate that learning is an active, not a passive process. Therefore, a writer's workshop (or lesson in composition) should involve the children in as much action as possible. Also, we infer from a study by Graves (1975) that an informal environment is more conducive to writing at greater length than a formal environment. Another study indicates that there is a relationship among the types of questions, stimuli, and the oral language production of children (Smith, 1977).

At this point we knew that our plan for prewriting activities would include oral activities which would actively involve the children in an informal environment.

From the studies of Britton (1975) and from the analysis of the writing process by Finder (1976) it seems clear that an awareness of the purpose of and the audience for a piece of writing definitely guides the process of composing and improves the product.

We also know from the work of Gagne (1965) and many others that concepts are transferable. We know that children learn from each other as well as from a teacher. Therefore, it seemed that if the purpose of each activity were clear, that the concept of, for example, supporting a statement with reasons, details or example were present in each activity, if the children did at least some group work, and if they knew the audience for each product, their writing workshop would be a true learning experience for them, for their teachers, and for us.

Lastly, we knew one thing we would *not* include in our workshop, and that was grammar exercises. Many studies over the years, more recently those of Elley (1976) and Harris (1962), indicate the grammar exercises do not contribute to the development of writing skills, whatever they might do for the convenience of the teacher in red-penciling the composition.

With some knowledge and many assumptions about what students can do in written composition, and with the objectives the teachers wished covered, we planned our workshop-teaching demonstrations for the 180 children we would see during the course of the day.

The plans for each grade were similar in that they went from oral to written work, included visual stimuli, included children working in groups as well as individually, and made clear that for some of the writing the audience would be their peers and for another piece, we, the workshop leaders, would be the audience. What follows is the specific account of the workshop for the 60 sixth grade children.

We decided to start the lesson in the cafeteria where we could work with sixty students for approximately sixty minutes. We began with a very brief introduction and an overview of the lesson itself. The actual lesson to meet the objective -- Write a topic sentence wth supporting details -- started wth two oral exercises.

The first exercise required students to complete the following statement: I like .... because. We used several different words to fill in the blank. Ice cream, vacation, T.V., morning, and animals were inserted to elicit responses from the students. We used the same statement with several students, and then repeated the various answers given by them in order to illustrate that a number of details could be given to support the statement. In addition we began to show that the reasons could be combined to support the original statement. In this exercise, students had an opportunity to express ideas orally, to share responses, and to work with the idea of statement and supporting detail.

Next we gave students an opportunity to examine a lump of clay. They touched it, smelled it, inspected it, played with it, some even tasted it. Then each student had to complete the following statement: Clay is .... In addition to supplying a word completion for the blank, each had to give three reasons for the word choice. When a student could not give three reasons, other students often volunteered reasons. As you can imagine, sixth graders had no difficulty in supplying a number of words to complete that sentence. In each case however, we required at least three reasons for the word choice.

In both of these exercises, the oral activity had involved students in thinking process and had given them an experience to which they could relate. Students had had the opportunity to share, to interact, and to learn from each other. Both exercises were non-threatening. Both served as prewriting exercises, developing concepts and ideas which would be used when the student finally put pencil to paper.

Neither of the two classes had ever worked in groups before the composition work. The next phase of our lesson not only gave students this opportunity but moved them toward meeting the objective as well.

We divided the two classes into twelve groups of five students each. We then briefly discussed advertisements, something with which students had some familiarity. They knew that a product was described, in addition reasons were given for purchasing the product. (Advertisements are our contemporary examples of the organizational pattern of topic with supporting details.) We decided that students knew enough about the advertisement format to prepare one of their own.

Each group received a card which had three suggested products for advertisement. Each group had to select one of the three. The products were such things as a box of mud, a homework robot, gloves with six fingers, a bag of square marbles, and a tennis racket with no strings.

Group interaction and discussion skills involved each student in each group as the group decided which product to advertise. Once the product was decided upon, reasons had to be listed to convience other students to buy the product (Purpose and audience are highlighted here).

Advertisement of the product had to include a drawing. Students roughed out their work and then transferred their ads to large sheets of newsprint. They used magic markers and crayons to make their ads visually attractive.

The groups worked diligently to prepare their ads. Their ideas were unique and illustrated that at this stage they grasped the idea of the lesson's objective. By far the most popular products were the homework machine and the six-finger glove.

The group presented its advertisements orally to the whole class. Each group was aided by the prepared visual which advertised the product. As teachers, we tried to get them to focus on the idea of topic and supporting details.

We had had the students involved in prewriting, oral activities, group work, concern for audience, and an active learning situation. It was now time to determine whether the concepts learned were transferable to individual work.

We gave each class a poster which it took back to its room. Each student had to look at the poster and write a letter to use to explain what the poster meant and to also give details to support the meaning. (One poster was a picture of a rabbit with this caption, "It's good to be petted a little, praised a little, appreciated a little." (#892 Argus Communication, Niles, Illinois, 1974.) The other poster was of two penquins with the caption, "When in doubt, do the friendliest thing." (#2136 Argus Communication, 1975).

The samples are exactly as received, errors and all. Personal identification has been removed for this article which accounts for incomplete letter form and a disjointed appearance.

The letters of three of the students follow:

Dean

I think the poster means love, respect, and gratefulness. If you are loved you will be happy and probably get along with other people. If you're respected you may be treated like a person and not be taken advantage of. If people are grateful to you then you can feel you accomplished something and possibly may like you own way. If people aren't grateful, respectful, and don't love you then you won't be a happy person.

Sincerely Yours,
Ray

Dear

When you were at the workshop Wednesday, you gave our teacher a poster with a picture and a saying and you asked us what the poster meant and give three reasons why it means that. The picture was of a rabbit and the saying said, It is good to be petted a little, and appreciated a little. I think it means that to be petted a little is to show love or favor, to be praised a little means that if you do a good job on something and somebody says, "Gee, that was a good job!" Then the saying says to be appreciated a little is when you give thanks to someone when they did something for you. One of the reasons why it meant that you show favor because it shows how much you care for that person or pet. Another reason is that if you give someone praise it gives them more enthusiasm and maybe they'll do a good job next time. The third reason is that you appreciate someone by saying "Thanks" or "That was great!" makes you and the other person feel a lot better.

Sincerely,

Paul

Dear

The message the poster gives me is that it's good someone cares for you. That's important because if no one cared or praised you, you would always be torn apart and thinking you do everything wrong. It's good to be petted and loved. If no one loved you, you would be dreadfully alone all the time. It's good to be appreciated and not taken for granted. No one likes it if they do nice things for someone all the time and they don't get thanked for it.

It was very kind of you to share your time and knowledge with us yesterday. I found it a worthwhile experience and I learned to give reasons when I state something. It was fun at the workshop and watching myself.

Yours truly,
Duncan

As can be seen from these samples, students were able to meet the objective. Of course, as in any class, some had more success than others; however, these letters could easily serve as the basis of the next lesson to meet the objectives -- which students needed continued work to better master the objective, and which students could benefit by moving to another objective. In addition, the students' writings could be used as a basis from which to teach word choice, detail selection, spelling, mechanics, individual perceptual response, and a number of other things as well.

What we and the teachers learned from the writer's workshop supported out original assumptions in the planning stage. Oral prewriting activities appeared to establish the concept we wished to teach and also actively involved the children in the learning process. The group writing experience provided students with an opportunity for interaction, work with a concept, and preparation of material for an audience of peers. This anticipated audience made students excited about doing a good job, which in turn influenced the creativeness, visual appeal, and correctness of the work itself.

In most cases, the concept of supporting a statement with appropriate details, reasons, or example was transferred to individual work. The time spent on prewriting activities proved to be profitable.

Both we and the teacher were surprised and pleased with the quality of the product in all three grades.

The teachers have since adopted this type of approach to written composition and report that their students remain enthusiastic about writing, write more, and that their writing is improving.

Bibliography

Britton, James, *et. al. The Development of Writing Abilities (11-18).* London: Macmillan Education, 1975.

Elley, W. B. *et al.* "The Role of Grammar in a Secondary School English Curriculum." *Research in the Teaching of English,* 1976, 10, 5-21.

Finder, Morris. *Reason and Art in Teaching Secondary-School English.* Philadelphia: Temple University Press, 1976.

Gagne, Robert M. *The Conditions of Learning.* New York: Holt, Rinehart and Winston, Inc., 1965.

Graves, Donald H. "An Examination of the Writing Processes of Seven Year Old Children." *Research in the Teaching of English,* 1976, 9, 227-241.

Harris, Roland Jr. "An Experimental Inquiry into the Functions and the Value of Formal Grammar in the Teaching of English, with Special Reference to the Teaching of Correct Written English to Children Aged Twelve to Fourteen." Unpublished. Ph.D. dissertation, etc., University of London, 1962.

Loban, Walter. *Language Development: Kindergarten Through Grade Twelve.* Urbana: National Council of Teachers of English, 1976.

Ludsteen, Sara W. *Children Learn to Communicate.* Englewood Cliffs: Prentice Hall, Inc., 1976.

Smith, Charlotte T. "The Relationship Between the Type of Questions, Stimuli, and the Oral Language Production of Children." *Research in the Teaching of English,* 1977, 2, 111-116.

*Adapted from article in *Indiana English,* Volume 3, Number 3-4, Spring, 1980.

SPECULATIONS ABOUT STUDENT WRITING AS SEEN ON STATEWIDE TESTS

Sheila A. Schlawin
State Education Department

We in the Bureau of Reading and English Education are in a position to see samples of student writing at many different levels, at least writing done in a test or test-like situation. Because of the statewide tests and the pretesting of questions in preparation for statewide tests, we have samples of writing available to us from students in all the grades from second through twelfth. We do not have time to analyze all the data, but certain generalizations seem to reoccur each year, especially from the various administrations of the Regents Comprehensive Examination in English and from the Regents Competency Test in Writing.

The very best student writers delight in taking a mundane topic on an examination, such as "Challenges" or "The Longest Day," and giving it a creative twist that lifts the essay or narrative above the run-of-the-mill response. The very best student writers, like the very best adult writers, have a voice, a persona, that is communicated, even in a test situation. Such writers are to be cherished and encouraged. The writer can take a topic such as "Time Capsule: 2999 A.D." and create a narrative that owes little to the current cliche[1] of science fiction, or create an essay that is a thoughtful extrapolation of trends that are apparent in our present society.

We are often delighted and encouraged at what the best student writers can do. One surprising indication of maturity that one of the best student writers exhibit is the ability to distance themselves from a situation in order to look at it objectively, and to maintain an objective tone throughout. Others exhibit the ability to maintain an ironic tone or sometimes even an appealing blend of irony and affection, for example in compositions dealing with some aspect of family or friendship.

Organization is also a strong feature of the best student writing. Although even mediocre writers seem to be able to organize a piece chronologically, the best writers seem to have additional methods of organization in their repertoire, such as cause and effect, reason and examples, statement and supporting detail.

Good student writers seem to be able to develop a piece adequately, even in a test situation, whether the piece is a literary essay, a personal essay or a persuasive essay. The good writer will take a topic such as "Human Rights for All Human Begins," and, instead of a pious, but vague homily, illustrate the points by referring to specific examples, whether from personal experience or from reading. The best writers on the Regents Competency Test in Writing can take a topic, for example, the introduction of a typing course as a high school graduation requirement, and not only state an opinion clearly, but also give excellent and persuasive reasons for the opinion, sometimes reasons which had not occurred to the adult model writer.

Not only do good student writers exhibit relatively little trouble with usage and mechanics, but they also demonstrate the ability to imbed phrases and clauses, to subordinate, and to use parallel construction. The following is an excerpt from a student essay:

> He would bring back a deer all by himself, and gain the respect of the men of the fort, the gratitude of the hungry he would feed, and, especially, the confidence of his mother.

On the other hand, even good student writers take few risks in a test-taking situation; caution is certainly understandable under the circumstances. However, this caution does lead to formula writing. Whole batches of papers from particular schools will begin and end the same way. Such caution also often leads to cliche's and triteness, although we teachers need to remember that sometimes what is stale and trite to us is new to students. Of course, the tests themselves at times encourage cliche's and triteness by such topics as "TV Commercials I'd Like to Rewrite," and "Challenges." A topic such as "Refugee Children" invariably seems to elicit a holier-than-thou attitude from the student writers. Many times the discussions are not on a level commensurate with the life experience or maturity of thought of eleventh grade students. The very fact that students tend to choose the "safe" topics; that is, the ones that can not easily be treated in a mundane way, gives us food for thought. Sometimes we feel that the fact that mediocrity is often rewarded by high grades is an encouragement of triteness and predictability. On the whole, we as teachers often teach students, particularly the better students, not to experiment, not to take risks, whether or not they are in a test-taking situation. We may not do this overtly, but teach it as a sort of subliminal message by giving formulas for the five paragraph essay, or by appearing to prefer correct, but lifeless, writing over lively, but flawed writing.

Few students taking the Regents Comprehensive Examination in English choose topics which require them to write a dialogue, a monologue, a script, a series of journal entries, or anything else which is a deviation from the three, four, or five paragraph essay. When they do choose them, the students do not seem to be able to handle the forms. For example, the responses to a topic which asked the student to write a dialogue between a parent and a teenager about peer pressures indicated that the writing task was totally beyond the capabilities of the students. On another test, papers of students who chose to write an interior monologue about the actions of a person observed on a bus indicated a lack of familiarity with the form and also a lack of invention of descriptive detail. We in the Bureau of English Education are trying to encourage implementation of the National Council of Teachers of English guideline:

Students write in many forms (e.g., essays, notes, summaries, poems letters, stories, reports, scripts, journals).

The results of such encouragement are not yet

apparent, at least on the Regents Comprehensive Examination in English.

From the previous discussion, it is apparent that student writing, whether good, bad, or indifferent, gives as much information about the way writing is taught as it does about the abilities of the students. Of course, the two aspects are inseparable. Compositions written for the Regents Comprehensive Examination in English and persuasive essays written for the Regents Competency Test in Writing suggest that many teachers are not helping students consider the audience for whom the piece is intended. It seems that in spite of research on the importance of audience, that a majority of students are more accustomed to writing to the teachers as examiners than they are to writing with a designated audience in mind. It may be argued that the students are merely being realistic; they know that no matter who the designated audience is supposed to be, it is the teachers who will be grading the paper. People who are familiar with the Competency Test know that there is a designated audience for each piece: for the business letter, the addressee; for the report, usually the class or a school newspaper or booklet, for the persuasive essay, a person or group of people to be persuaded. On the whole, more students who take the Regents Competency Test in Writing seem to be able to adjust the persuasive essay to the designated audience than students seem to be able to adjust to a designated audience on the Comprehensive Examination. Is this because it is a persuasive essay or because teacher and students know there will be a designated audience for this writing?

It does seem significant that the great majority of students who take the Comprehensive Examination choose a topic with no designated audience. In the June, 1980 Regents Comprehensive 79.1% of the sample of papers studied had essays from the following list of topics presented as a list:

> Challenges
> The world over a barrel (of oil)
> The refugee children
> T.V. Commercials I'd like to rewrite
> When dreams and reality collide
> Human rights for all human beings
> Applause, please!
> The Muppets

Not only that, no particular audience seemed to be in mind when the piece was written.

Two of the other three choices on the examination invovled a designated audience, but the audience factor did not seem to be handled well.

Admittedly, a test situation is an artificial one, and may not be a true picture of whether students can write to an audience other than the teacher as rater. We do suggest that English departments in schools evaluate their own programs according to the National Council of Teachers of English guideline:

> Students write for a variety of audiences (e.g.,
> self, classmates, the community, the teacher)
> to learn that approaches vary.

Various national surveys have indicated that most of the writing in high school English classes is done in connection with literature. If this is true, then some of the responses to the literary essay questions are surprising. Although the best responses are indicative of insight into the piece being discussed, give reasons and details from the piece to support generalizations, and are well organized, too many students give only plot summaries as the essay. It is difficult to teach students to analyze literature and choose the elements that are suitable for the discusion of one particular aspect. Yet it is surprising that more students don't do a better job of it when we consider the concentration on literature in most high school English classes.

For example, we consider essays that were written in response to the following questions:

105

> In literature there are many characters who do not compromise their principles. From the biographies, novels, and full-length plays you have read, choose a total of two works. For each work, identify a character. Then indicate the principle in which the charater believed, and show, by specific references, that the actions of the character upheld this principle. Give titles and authors.
>
> Suffering can be a challenge to grow or an occasion to surrender to defeat. From the plays, novels, biographies, and books of true experience you have read, choose two. For each, choose one character who had to cope with a crucial, painful experience. Describe the experience for each and tell how it became a challenge or an occasion to surrender. In each case, show the effect the response had on his/her life. Give titles and authors.

The majority of students did not focus on either the principles as in the first question or on the suffering as in the second. Instead of selecting the actions which upheld the principles of the characters, students tended to summarize the entire plot. The same was true of the second question -- the entire plot instead of the crucial experience and its effect on the character.

Another interesting aspect of the essays written for the literature part of the Regents Comprehensive is that year after year, *Macbeth* can be made to fit anything. Macbeth did not compromise his principles; he kept on killing. Macbeth met the challenge of the witches, of Banquo, of MacDuff. Macbeth came through even in the following topic:

> In literary works there may appear a person who dares to fight the established system of society and stand up for what he or she believes. From the full-length plays, novels, and books of true experience you have read, choose two. Identify a character for each work and explain the cause for which the character was fighting. By using specific references, describe the actions of the characters and the results, good or bad, of the actions.

We were surprised to learn from several students that Macbeth was fighting for a cause. He was fighting the establishment by killing the king. Somehow none of these students explained away why, in that case, he so quickly assumed the kingship himself.

In spite of the multipurpose *Macbeth*, we are impressed by the variety of works that are used, and used suitably, in response to the literature question. What many students seem to need is more help in focusing on the relevant aspects of the question. We suspect that students need help in focusing on aspects relevant to a central idea whether they are writing a test essay or not.

It will be no revelation to any English teacher that a common problem in the student writing that we see is a lack of specificity. Statements are made without details, reasons, or examples to support the statements. Even when a personal experience is being related, the student tells rather than shows: "I was embarrassed," for example, instead of "I could feel my face getting hot and red and I looked over his shoulder in order not to have to meet his eyes."

Maintaining a point of view throughout a piece is another problem for many student writers. For example, a student may relate the death of a person from whose point of view a story is told and then shift to a survivor's point of view for the last paragraph, or relate a father's return, mixing the child's and father's point of view. Sometimes there will be an inconsistency such as "Long ago she was loved, everyone looked up to her, she always had a shoulder to cry on."

Sometimes even good students who are trying hard fall into traps such as the following: "Gradually opening my encrusted eyes, the glowing digits read 5:30 a.m."

Poor writers, both on the Comprehensive and the Competency tests, have all the familiar problems of content, development and organization, and struggle with usage, mechanics and spelling as well.

The student writing we see on tests leads us back to the recommendations we have so often made or endorsed:

1) Students should be given the opportunity to write and helped to write for many different purposes, for many different audiences, and in different genres. We notice that on the Regents Comprehensive Examination in English, even good student writers do not seem to be able to handle such forms as journal entries, monologues, dialogues, or scripts. They seem to need more practice in writing for different audiences. In school situations, as contrasted with test situations, the audiences should be real as often as possible.

2) As from time immemorial, we need to stress adequate development of a composition with specifics, details, examples, reasons. Peer conferencing may be more helpful in this aspect of writing than it often is in the proofreading aspect. Perhaps we as teachers are sometimes too easily satisfied with the content of a piece of writing if the mechanics and spelling are adequate.

3) We should teach students more about how to go about revising and rewriting a composition. It seems to us, from looking at first and final drafts, that most students merely recopy without making improvements; in fact, sometimes making the final draft worse than the first. Many have not learned that revising is more than correcting errors.

We at the Bureau do see hope for the prospect of student writing improving and continuing to improve in the future. Already it seems that more students can write at least passably as shown by the latest competency test. With increased knowledge about teaching writing and increased emphasis on the teaching of writing, more students will not only write passably, but will write well. Above all, let us remember that

"Reading" and "Writing" are meaningless as well as disembodied if they are regarded as ends in themselves, not as means of learning, imagining, communicating, thinking, remembering, and understanding.*

*Glenda L. Bissex, *GNYS AT WRK: A Child Learns to Write and Read*, Cambridge, Harvard University Press, 1980, p. 1.

III. PROGRAM

THE PROGRAM FOR EFFECTIVE WRITING: HOW TO ESTABLISH IT, HOW TO CONTROL IT

Kenneth Kahn

Dutchess County BOCES

Much is being said in current literature and on the conference circuit about the teaching of writing and the development of writing programs. We read and hear that much energy and many dollars are being expended on the "writing problems" as schools respond to the pressures from all sources to improve their writing programs, improve instruction, and develop effective management systems. While schools are showing a wide range of expertise and sophistication in their approaches to defining their needs, planning their programs and establishing and attaining their objectives, there is evidence that these same schools have not yet understood the elements of program management or the interrelationships among the elements, a necessary understanding if the schools are to achieve good management. It is the need to identify program elements and to understand their interrelationships in developing and managing effective writing programs that is subject of this article.

Let us begin to address the problem with a couple of generally accepted notions about problems with education today and the importance of good management.

The first notion, derived from surveys conducted by Gallup, Peat, Marwick, Mitchell & Co., and other organizations, is that schools suffer, among other problems, from poor teaching, from lack of well-defined educational goals, and from poor educational management.

A second notion is that a district that systematically dedicates resources and staff to change and to control its administrative, curriculuar, instructional and management practices to attain its educational objectives is more likely to be successful than the district that has no such dedication.

In a recent article entitled, "Effective Ways to Improve Public Education," by Dr. Fenwick English,[7] Director of Educational Consulting, Peat, Marwick, Mitchel & Co, the author reports statistical data from their surveys and describes several approaches to deal with these problems.

His first point is that the well-managed district (and the one more likely to have a well-managed writing program) is characterized by close adherence to five basic standards. These include:

1. Evidence of system control of resources, programs and personnel (If no one is in charge, everyone is in charge).
2. Clear objectives for students and performance measures - as basis for resource allocation.
3. Data base related to program development, implementation and performance. This includes data and records re: program planning and operating decisions.
4. Use of pupil results to improve programs or to decide to drop particular programs. This includes coding and examination of test results for use in program decisions.
5. Ability to achieve a desired level of performance within a defined level of support.

The key elements, according to Dr. English, are the ability by the system to demonstrate control of its direction and to change direction when necessary. This ability to control requires clear objectives, pupil standards, assessment data and consistency of district staff in following the agreed upon policies and directions.

The critical relationships are among what teachers are teaching (content -- or the description of the real curriculum), what pupils are learning (the testing program), and what pupils are supposed to be learning (the curriculum guide or the prescription). *Curriculum power*, reaching the desired outcomes, depends on the degree to which these elements coincide. (Figure 1.)

Figure 1

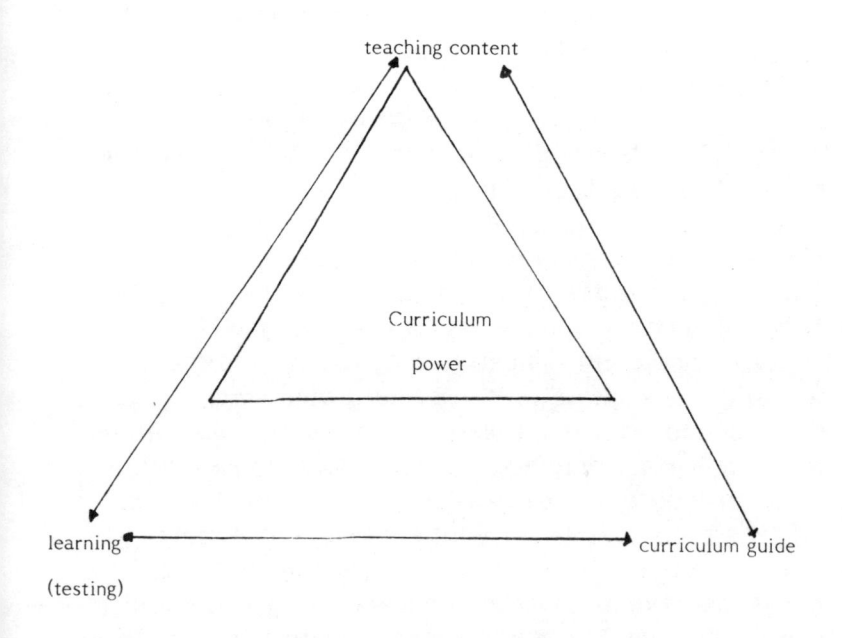

```
                    teaching content


                     Curriculum
                       power


  learning ←——————————————————→ curriculum guide
  (testing)
```

English goes on to say that in order to improve the effectiveness and efficiency of an educational program, a school district must be able to bring about changes in the interrelationships. In creating a new writing program, the district would be wise to build in congruences at the outset. This requires clear understanding of the aims, purposes and outcomes to be achieved; the determination of what is to be taught; auditing to assure that teachers are, in fact, teaching what is intended and are consistently following the directions from the decision makers.

Where gaps occur between what teachers teach and what they are supposed to teach, we have program variance. Some variance is not harmful and may, in fact, be healthy. Three areas of variance are important in achieving maximum curriculum power.

The first two are the *content of teaching* and the *time spent* on the content or *level of repetition* tied to the content. The third is the *sequence* or order of presentation - within a grade or from grade level to grade level. It is thus related to time spent and level of repetition and states a ratio between what is taught and how much time is spent teaching it. Variance may be measured horizontally on any grade level or vertically, K-12.

Variance can be illustrated by comparing the content of two teachers on the same grade level who are supposed to teach a one week unit on writing *persuasive discourse.* Both may teach the unit with 100% congruence on "content." However, one may spend one week and the other ten weeks with a variance of time at ten times greater for one teacher than the other. One teacher may spend a week on examining, and using as a model, a series of fables. The other teacher may deal with editorials, advertising and fables with at least one writing task each week.

The extent to which the school district knows the degrees to which staff is consistently carrying out its directions is a major part in controlling its direction and achieving maximum curriculum power.

The technique of discovering degrees of congruence or variance is called *Curriculum Mapping*.[9] Developing a map requires each teacher to indicate what it is he or she is teaching in units selected for the map. The content may consist both of the subject matter and whatever else children are expected to learn; skills, processes, attitudes. The teacher also indicates how much time, in hours or weeks, he or she spends on various parts of the content.

The comparing of individual teacher's maps generates a content and teacher chart that will clearly indicate congruence or variance between teachers regarding what they teach. A comparison of time spent by each teacher provides the *time on task* variance.

The illustration in Figure 2 should help make this more understandable. Borrowing from the article "Curriculum Mapping" by Fenwich English, *Educational Leadership,* April 1980,[9] we see a map created by one of five teachers of fifth grade social studies. Let us suppose that all five teachers developed maps and the following data were generated:

1. The *actual social studies* curriculum for all of the fifth grade units described by the 5 teachers consisted of 20 content topics.
2. Only five of the 20 topics were taught by all 5 teachers.
3. Three topics were taught by only 2 teachers.
4. Twelve topics were taught by only one teacher.

It is possible, according to this data, that for pupils in different classes, by the end of the fifth grade, that the curriculum content could have a 60% variance or difference of 12 topics.

FIGURE 2
SAMPLE CLASSROOM CURRICULUM MAP
FIFTH GRADE SOCIAL STUDIES(9)

THE CONTEXT/CONTENT OF THE CLASSROOM/U.S. HISTORY			
My fifth grade social studies program begins with the early explorers of our nation. These include the Portuguese explorers and Columbus. We study the conquest of Mexico and the Incas. We examine the evolution of religious freedom in the U.S. by studying Lord Baltimore's development of Maryland and the Act of Toleration of 1649. We also model for a week a "mock" House of Burgess of Virginia. We also set up a unit on the old Southern Planation and its economy.			TIME A 4
CONCEPTS	SKILLS	ATTITUDES	
-Understand the impact on the New World of Puritan Migration of 1600-40; -Understand the trials of Roger Williams in moving to Rhode Island	-Be able to write stories based on the explorations -Be able to use the necessary resources to do good seat work -Work with other students in the House of Burgess	-Develop respect for the diversity of opinions about life & religion; -Awareness of the need for a proper forum for dialogue to occur about sensitive issues.	TOTAL TIME B
TIME 1.50	TIME 2.00	TIME .50	4
GEOGRAPHY I teach the geography of the U.S. by working with four different kinds of maps; relief, landform, political, and historical. The students work in committees and develop one of each for a time period they select.			TIME A .50
CONCEPTS	SKILLS	ATTITUDES	
-Understand the use of time belts; -Use longitude and latitude to locat cities & places -Understand the International Data Line	-Use string to measure distances on the globe -Make time estimates of how long it will take to reach a place by various methods	-Awareness of the need for international agreement on dates and time -Awareness of the need for uniformly understood may symbols	TIME B
TIME .20	TIME .25	TIME .05	.50
CONTEMPORARY U.S. CITY LIFE My study of city life involves an analysis of five great American cities: New York, Chicago, Los Angeles, Boston and New Orleans as to quality of life, schools, jobs, problems, newspapers, law enforcement and history.			TIME A .50
CONCEPTS	SKILLS	ATTITUDES	
-Due to the linkages between cities by modern transportation and, problems are very similar despite geographical distances involved;	-Ability to use a variety of contemporary periodical literature and categorize in report form as required;	-Awareness that modern problems in the cities are indeed complex and are not resolved by dealing with possible solutions in isolation from each other.	TIME B
TIME .10	TIME .35	TIME .05	.50
TOTAL TIME 1.80	TOTAL TIME 2.60	TOTAL TIME .60	TOTAL 5

A second major tool is needed at the outset to help the district establish what is to be taught in order to carry out district and state mandates and requirements and to maintain its ability to control its operations.

This tool is an *intent structure* or *objective tree* ([12], [19]) which *identifies and relates the elements of program content* and *program structure.* The concept is derived from engineering, the mathematical and computer concepts in which a set of directed graphs, binary relationships and networks result in a heirarchical arrangement of elements ([10], [17]) showing superordinate/subordinate relationships. It identifies higher order objectives, supporting objectives, and associated objectives and the relationships among them. the resulting engineering structure is called an "objective tree."

The Objective Tree For A Writing Program is such an intent structure. It identifies the purposes, goals, objectives and content areas of the *writing improvement program* that may be developed by any district. It also provides a sense of heirarchy of superordinate goals and subordinate goals and supportive objectives. It relates program goals to program objectives and program objectives to instructional objectives. It shows "why" we do we do, as well as "how" we can achieve our higher level of objectives. [11, 12, 19]

The "Tree" will enable the observer to appreciably enhance his or her understanding of the content[12] of the entire writing program, and provides the basis for the development of lessons and units to provide the instruction to meet the objective requirements.[9] These will be determined by the sequence of specific objectives as developed in each district; they will give a clear understanding of what is to be taught, when is it to be taught, why it is to be taught, and how the teaching relates to the overall purposes. The teacher is in a better position to provide instruction that is more naturally related to and supportive of the overall program goals and directions.

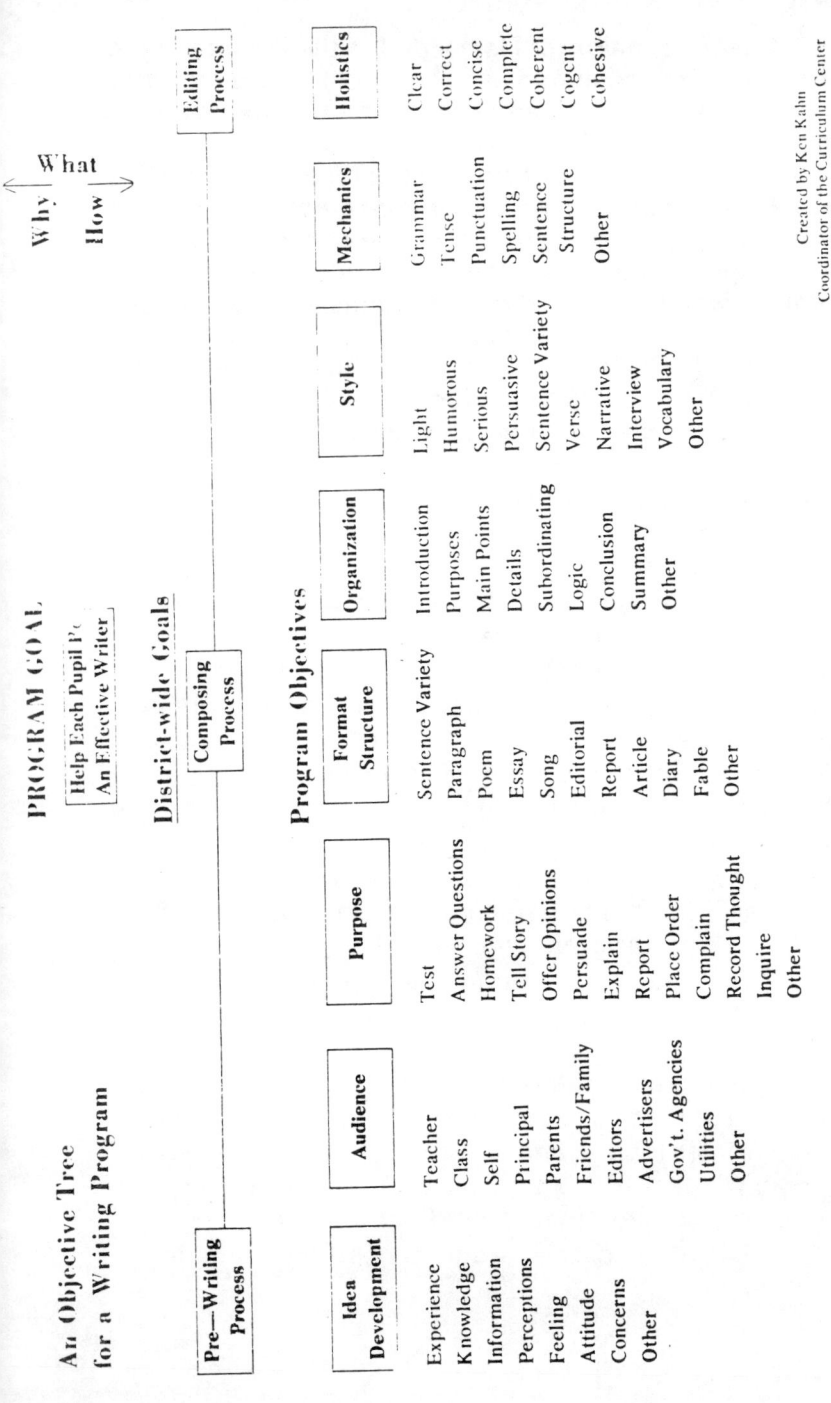

An Objective Tree for a Writing Program

PROGRAM GOAL

Help Each Pupil Be An Effective Writer

Why / What / How

District-wide Goals

- Pre—Writing Process
- Composing Process
- Editing Process

Program Objectives

Idea Development
- Experience
- Knowledge
- Information
- Perceptions
- Feeling
- Attitude
- Concerns
- Other

Audience
- Teacher
- Class
- Self
- Principal
- Parents
- Friends/Family
- Editors
- Advertisers
- Gov't. Agencies
- Utilities
- Other

Purpose
- Test
- Answer Questions
- Homework
- Tell Story
- Offer Opinions
- Persuade
- Explain
- Report
- Place Order
- Complain
- Record Thought
- Inquire
- Other

Format Structure
- Sentence Variety
- Paragraph
- Poem
- Essay
- Song
- Editorial
- Report
- Article
- Diary
- Fable
- Other

Organization
- Introduction
- Purposes
- Main Points
- Details
- Subordinating
- Logic
- Conclusion
- Summary
- Other

Style
- Light
- Humorous
- Serious
- Persuasive
- Sentence Variety
- Verse
- Narrative
- Interview
- Vocabulary
- Other

Mechanics
- Grammar
- Tense
- Punctuation
- Spelling
- Sentence Structure
- Other

Holistics
- Clear
- Correct
- Concise
- Complete
- Coherent
- Cogent
- Cohesive

INSTRUCTIONAL STRATEGIES

For each item in the section above, the teacher may develop instructional objectives and lessons or units to implement instruction.

Created by Ken Kahn
Coordinator of the Curriculum Center
Dutchess County BOCES

Understanding and using an "Objective Tree" can be extremely useful in moving a program towards its desired outcomes because the very process of learning to use it provides staff with an agreed upon set of major goals and objectives and a solid base upon which to build strategies for implementation. [11, 14, 19] With experience, staff members can identify needs or gaps in their own teaching approaches. In addition, staff can determine whether certain aspects are overemphasized or are unnecessarily duplicated.[14] Areas identified as needs or concerns may be addressed by building-level or grade-level teams as well as by individuals. In addition, items on the tree may serve as an evaluative check list.

The concept was created and developed by Dr. John W. Warfield, chairman of the Electrical Engineering Department, University of Virginia, who was at the time senior research leader, at Battelle, in the development and application of systems methodologies to complex societal problems, particularly "Interpretive Structural Modeling."[25-26] Dr. Warfield based his work on several simple notions:

First, the findings by psychologists reported by Simon indicate that the short term memory capacity of most people is in the range of 5-7 "chunks" of information (elements plus their relationships). In order to deal with problems consisting of more than this range, we need tools or models.[1]

Second, even simple problems have several elements. Complex problems have more elements and more intricate relations among them. In simple problems it is fairly easy to understand the chunks and arrive at suitable solutions. In complex problems, with many elements and a maze of interactions, solutions are not so obvious.

For example, Waller[24] points out that in a problem of priority-setting involving only three goals, there are 13 possible ways in which they may be ranked. These possibilities are shown in Figure 3 in which A, B, and C represent three different goals.

FIGURE 3

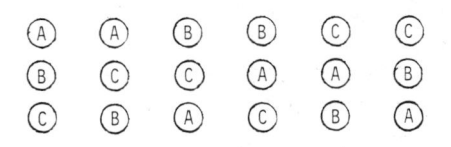

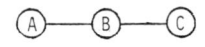

FIGURE 3

The complexity of the problem escalates to astronomical proportions with the addition of only a few more elements. For example, with just 15 elements there are approximately 1.3 trillion (1,300,000,000,000) ways in which a strong ordering like that in the upper part of figure 3 can be achieved, and this does not include the possibilities where multiple elements occur on a given level such as in the second row.

The need exits, then, for a tool to arrive at solutions. This tool is known as the Interpretive Structural Model, an example of which is the *Objective Tree for a Writing Program.*

The process utilized in developing the writing tree has several important steps.

First is to arrive at a clear understanding and definition of the problem so that we can direct our efforts toward adequate solutions and be able to recognize parallel, subordinated or related problems without being accidentally side-tracked.[1, 11, 12, 14]

Second (and not necessarily in this numerical order) is the need to identify and list the elements that constitute the problem. This usually depends on a combination of our own knowledge and what we derive from reading or research,[12] and will include not only program content items (or *what is to be taught* but purpose items as well (goals, objectives...).

Please note here that we have to distinguish between the "societal problem" (need for a writing program) and the more immediate problem of designing the tool to solve the societal problem (the intent structure). In carrying out the second step of identifying the content and purpose elements, reference was made to the Bureau of English Education's two publications: *The Manual for Administrators and Teachers* and *Helping Student Writers*[4] and the National Council's *Standard for Basic Skills Writing Program*[23] and articles by James Squire[22] and Cecelia Kingston[16] and references to Charles Cooper, Lee Odell[5,6] and other research writers. These courses provide the content element of a writing program.

This leads to the third step. This is the determination of placement of items in the structure so that a heirarchy of goals, objectives and supportive or related items may be designed. To do this, four questions must be answered:[19]

   a. What is the over-arching purpose for this writing program? (Program goals)
   b. What are the long-term objectives or program directions required if we are to arrive at the higher goals? What are the objectives for the writing program?
   c. What subordinate objectives are required to support the writing program's major objectives?
   d. What other, or associated, objectives are required to assist in achieving the major program objectives?

Developing the answers to these questions may be aided by using any of several techniques. One approach is to generate a list of elements of the problem (Step 1) and record each on a set of 3 x 5 cards.[8] Much time would be saved by using the items identified on the NCTE *Standards* or the *Manual* . . . (NYS . . . Test in Writing). Figure 4.

FIGURE 4
TENTATIVE LIST OF WRITING PROGRAM CONTENT ELEMENTS AND CONCERNS

- write well
- record thoughts . . .
- read back thoughts
- communicate
- develop literacy
- achieve purposes
- inform, notify
- entertain
- develop skills of rhetoric
- become a "published" person
- deliver "message"
- develop thoughts and ideas
- put ideas together
- correct writing errors
- identify superior objectives (mission, goals . . .)
- identify major goals, purposes
- identify (group with major goals . . .) subordniate or supportive items
- identify associated objectives (to attain program by)
- time on task
- use correct vocabulary
- write with logic and direction
- relating ideas
- subordinating thoughts
- use sentence variety

- ability to compose
- ability to revoke
- address audience
- write poetry
- write reports
- write letters
- write diaries
- persuade
- inquire
- complain
- suggest
- write a story
- write to relatives
- write to government
- write to agencies

- develop skill
- write in correct English

- organizing writing

- beginning
- main ideas
- conclusion
- summary
- outlining
- use proper grammar punctuation and mechanics

This results in a mix of goals, objectives, purposes, activities, processes, outcomes, approaches... The next step is to sort and classify the cards by broad or major categories and position items in terms of their relationships to major topics. ([12, 14, 16])

Determining relationships may be accomplished by starting with an item and asking the question "Why do I want to accomplish this?" By asking the "why" question repeatedly we arrive at our ultimate "why" or highest order objective. The intent structure derived in this way is generated in an upward direction.

By starting with the highest order objective and repeatedly asking "How will I achieve this?", the intent structure is generated in a "downward" direction ([12, 14, 19, 25, 26])

Following either the upward or downward procedure, or both at various points in the process, will lead to a tree with clear linkages between items. This process, if brought to completion, is an extremely time consuming one and WAS NOT CARRIED OUT IN THIS CASE. A decision, in the present case, was to present an intent structure portraying the elements and their relationships in a general rather than specified or tightly structured way. Anyone who wishes to complete the process by following the procedure outlined in this paper is welcome to do so. My own bias is that while a formal tree may be extremely useful, the usability of the present structure lies in its simplicity.

The Objective Tree for a Writing Program should be viewed as one component of a total educational program. This entire component may well fit under an even higher order objective that is itself one of several parallel objectives supporting the ultimate or highest order goal for our educational system. See the following illustration. (Figure 5.)

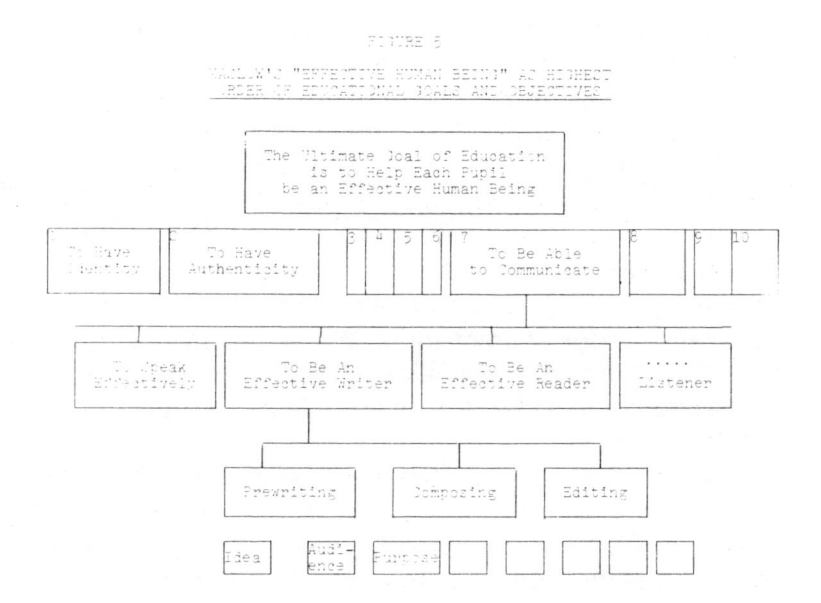

FIGURE 5

SHOWING "EFFECTIVE HUMAN BEING" AS HIGHEST ORDER OF EDUCATIONAL GOALS AND OBJECTIVES

```
         The Ultimate Goal of Education
              is to Help Each Pupil
           be an Effective Human Being
```

| To Have Identity | To Have Authenticity | 3 | 4 | 5 | 6 | 7 To Be Able to Communicate | 8 | 9 | 10 |

| To Speak Effectively | To Be An Effective Writer | To Be An Effective Reader | Listener |

| Prewriting | Composing | Editing |

| Idea | Audience | Purpose | | | | |

For illustrative purposes only, let us examine Maslow's concept of the "Effective Human Being."[15] If we borrow from this concept and accept the effective human being as the highest order goal of our educational system, we may then see the relationship of our entire tree to this highest order goal and at least one of the supportive objectives (#7 Communications) related to the entire educational system.

Maslow's model identifies ten characteristics of the effective human being:

1. identity
2. authenticity
3. open-mindednes
4. independence
5. responsibility
6. reason
* 7. communication
8. problem solving
9. compassion
10. zest for the everyday

Our illustration shows the heirarchical link from the highest order goal: "effective human being," to district-wide support goal: #7, "communication," to program goals: "effective writer," and thence to the supportive associated objectives for the writing program. Not developed in this illustration are the linkages between the highest order goal and the other 9 characteristics of the "effective human being." Nor are the downward linkages shown connecting the 9 other elements and the supportive elements for each of them. While it is important to recognize the place of the writing program within the entire educational structure, it is not feasible to portray it in this article.

In the "Writing Tree," the designation of the Prewriting, Composing and Editing Processes as the major program goals reflects the work of Charles Chew and Sheila Schlawin of the Bureau of English Education as seen in the Manual for Administrators and Teachers, [4] of Cecelia Kingston in "To Assign Is Not To Teach;"[15] and of

James Squire who emphasized the processes of writing as seen in his presentation, "The Collision of the Basics Movement with Current Research" ... presented to the Conference on "The English Curriculum Under Fire" ([22]) at the University of Chicago, in June 1978. Squire distinguishes between those skills that can be taught and mastered, grade by grade (grammar, usage . . .) and the writing process which are synthesis of skills and abilities and not so easily measured and which are not appreciably enhanced by mastery of "mastery type skills."

The designation as higher objectives for these processes is further supported by the National Council of Teachers of English in its definition of writing, recently presented in its "Standards for Basic Skills Writing Programs" (March 1979).

The Council offers the following as its operational definition of writing:

> Writing is the process of selecting, combining and developing ideas in effective sentences, paragraphs, and, often, longer units of discourse. The process requires the writer to cope with a number of variables: method of development (narrating, explaining, describing reporting and persuading); form report); purpose from discovering and expressing (from a limerick to a formal letter to a long research personal feelings and values to conducting the impersonal "business" of everyday life); possible audiences (oneself, classmates, a teacher, "the world"). Learning to write and to write increasingly well involves developing increasing skill and sensitivity in selecting from and combining these variables to shape particular messages. It also involves learning to conform to conventions of the printed language, appropriate to the age of the writer and to the form, purpose, and tone of the message.

Beyond the pragmatic purpose of shaping messages to others, writing can be a means of self-discovery, of finding out what we believe, know . . . and it warrants the full, generous and continuing effort of all teachers.

The *Processes* are the major *program goals*. Supporting them are a set of *program objectives*, each linked to the Process goals. The arrangement of items to the tree uses placement and proximity rather than linking lines to show relationships. *Idea development,* as a major program objective is placed nearest to the *Pre-Writing process* to show the logical sequential place in the writing program. Supporting "idea development" are several items that are illustrative rather than heirarchical.

An interesting diversion for the more serious practitioners of the art of objective tree development would be a reconfiguration of the major objective - *idea development* by placing it at the very bottom of the column. By going through the "why" process we can determine or generate a new major objective.*

Pre-Writing process

WHY

HOW

*To establish turf

To know and be sure

To firm up ideas

To explore and record feelings

To develop ideas

If, according to Donald Graves, being sure of one's turf, by idea development, is a major first step in the composing process, this change makes a great deal of sense. It is also consistent with the upward generation of an objective tree, and it permits direct linkage downward to an entire section on lesson development.

The placement of the program objectives dealing with the sense of audience, purposes, style, format and organization shows close relationships to the composing process, but acknowledges their relationship to the pre-writing process stage.

Why the placement of audience before purpose? I have no satisfactory answer for that since both are important determiners for style, format, vocabulary, etc. Whichever comes first, both are important and occupy logical places in the structure. As before, under each program objective are several items that are illustrative rather than heirarchical.

At the right of the structure are two elements that support the major goal of "editing." Graves, Chew, Schlawin, Squire, Braddock [2] *et al* indicate that grammar, usage and mechanics are the chief tools in the domain of editing. The final column lists the general reminders of what effective writing is supposed to be.

Putting the tree to work

If the structure does its work, it will enable the user to be familiar with (a) all aspects of a writing program; (b) the major purposes and goals of the program; (c) the direction the program is to take; (d) areas of emphasis or neglect in the present program: (e) what is to be taught; (f) evaluative criteria; (g) possible new directions; (h) ideas for additions to the structure - re: asociated objectives such as needs assessment, inservice training, curriculum mapping. . . .

The "tree" calls for, but does not address, the entire domain of teaching and managing instruction. The present "tree" might be expanded at a future time to deal with the *purposes and strategies of teaching* by creating an additional section of *associated objectives.* The importance of dealing with this area cannot be overestimated in strengthening the district's ability to demonstrate control in managing its programs.

In the work being carried on in developing writing programs, there is heavy emphasis, in both curriculum development and staff development, on the necessity for *teaching, not assigning,* as part of managing instruction in the process of writing. The case is made, most effectively, by Cecilia Kingston, former Coordinator of Language Arts, Public Schools of the Tarrytowns, The items on the objective tree are, in part, derived from her article, "To Assign Is Not To Teach."[15] The premise is that unless we plan, develop, implement and evaluate units of instruction on writing we are not likely to be any more successful than we have been. Most of us have "taught" English by assigning writing tasks and in most cases the assignments have been based on false assumptions about the learner, the clairty of the assignment, and the way in which a learner learns.

Mrs. Kingston continues with the proposition that the clearer and **more** specific the assignment, the most likely the attainment of better results, provided, of course, that the pupil has at hand all the information required to do the job. She contends that the quality of a writing product will be influenced by having (1) a sense of purpose; (2) a specific audience; (3) an understanding that what is being written will have a messsage for someone else; (4) a set of directions that is specific and limited in focus; (5) sufficient time for completing a first draft, for editing and for revising; and (6) interest in a meaningful (and attainable) task.

Cecelia Kingston's message is augmented by Jim Squire and others in their work dealing with "time on task."[9,22] Squire cites a great deal of research on the effectiveness of giving sufficient instructional time to attain instruction objectives. He agrees with Kingston on the need to provide models of excellence for study and examination so that students are familiar with criteria for satisfactory (or better) writing.

There is also need for time for drill and practice for writing, reading, and discussion, for exploration and questioning, for idea development and as Donald Graves[13] puts it, to attain the "arrogance of knowing." Graves points out the need to set up listening posts where small groups can read and listen to each other, question, probe, suggest, react.... He also emphasizes the importance of providing sufficient time to complete the writing tasks. As he tells audiences wherever and whenever he can, the British look with disdain on the American's concern both with grades and the need to hurry. Pupils, in the British program, are permitted time to think, feel, and develop their ideas; to compose and revise and to complete a piece of writing. In the view of British teachers, a pupil's writing is not "incorrect," it is merely "incomplete."

Accompanying the need for sufficient time is the

need for effective instruction. Charles Cooper and Lee Odell[5,6] deal with what should be taught in the pre-writing, composing and post-composing phases. Squire points out that the initial pre-composing phase is the period of invention and of planning; a period well suited for instruction in the basic crutches for planning - ways of paragraphing, outlining, using topic sentences, **considering one's point of view and the nature of one's audience.**[22]

The period of instruction in the composing phase requires the presence and involvement of the teacher and ample opportunity for writing to occur in class under the guidance, direction and supervision of the teacher. **It is at this time that pupils can be taught to become reflective writers, to plan ahead what they plan to say.**[12,22]

The editing phase requires instruction in the areas of improving content, organization, sentence structure and mechanics. It is in relation to improving a piece of writing that *mechanics* become *meaningful and important* - not, as is too often the case, as separate units or in conjunction with the composing process. Squire points out the substantial body of research that demonstrates conclusively the lack of relationship between the study of grammar and the ability to compose.[2,20] Thus the case is made for the direct relationship between mechanics and the editing process and reflection of this relationship on the "tree" by means of location and proximity.

FIGURE 6

"Tree" Section Depicting Possible Associated Objectives
in support of a Writing Program

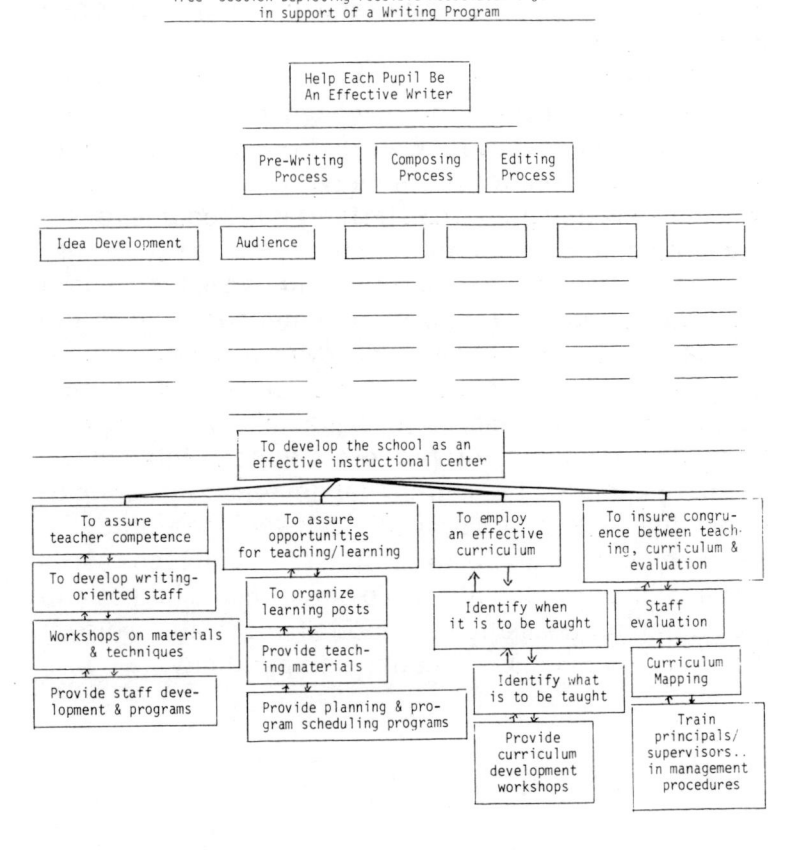

- Help Each Pupil Be An Effective Writer
  - Pre-Writing Process
  - Composing Process
  - Editing Process

- Idea Development
- Audience

To develop the school as an effective instructional center

- To assure teacher competence
  - To develop writing-oriented staff
  - Workshops on materials & techniques
  - Provide staff development & programs

- To assure opportunities for teaching/learning
  - To organize learning posts
  - Provide teaching materials
  - Provide planning & program scheduling programs

- To employ an effective curriculum
  - Identify when it is to be taught
  - Identify what is to be taught
  - Provide curriculum development workshops

- To insure congruence between teaching, curriculum & evaluation
  - Staff evaluation
  - Curriculum Mapping
  - Train principals/supervisors.. in management procedures

128

There remains still one more component that we might consider for inclusion on a more fully developed tree. This is the part that deals with the associated or other objectives required to assist in achieving the major program objectives. Most districts seem to be addressing this area by providing inservice training, curriculum development, establishing writing centers and providing a classroom environment more conducive to more effective teaching and learning in the area of writing. Current emphasis seems to be on developing curriculum guides related to writing in the various content areas, and then in providing staff development to help all staff use the approaches and strategies for teaching writing as an interdisciplinary concern. An important associated task is the staff training of principals, coordinators and supervisors in clinical supervision, staff evaluation and program evaluation. The Educational Performance Audit and particularly the curriculum map, suggested by Dr. Fenwick English, is a major tool available to carry forward this task by identifying the variances in curriculum, teaching and the specific needs for administrative training.

The items on the objective tree may well be the items against which actual teaching is checked for congruence in the mapping procedure to see if everyone is consistent in carrying out the prescribed program for the defined reasons.

Checking on congruences throughout the writing program, by grade level, by school...is a very important part of both program development and program evaluation.

If pupils are learning to write well and do well on competency and other tests, and if these results stem from effective teaching across the board in which what is supposed to be taught (the curriculum) is actually taught, we might well conclude that the program is an effective one and we would know why this was so.

In the same way, if pupils were writing well in

science, social studies, health, music . . . and the results stemmed from effective teaching we would have evidence of an effective program.

The importance of all of this is the ability of each student to become an effective writer. The task of getting each pupil from where he or she is to where he or she should be is the task of every teacher and administrator. The task will be immeasurably easier when an effective staff provides consistently effective programs. The tools for solving the problems of developing the effective program are emerging. It has been the contention in this paper that such tools are (a) *The Objective Tree* - to provide the curriculum planners and administrative and teaching staff the content, direction and structure of their writing program and (b) *The Educational Performance Audit* using curriculum maps to determine the degree to which staff is following directions and the degree to which the district is actually controlling its programs.

REFERENCES

Baldwin, Maynard M. ed. *Portraits of Complexity,* Battelle Monograph No. 9, Battelle Memorial Institute, Columbus, 1975.

Braddock, Richard et al., *Research in Written Composition,* Urbana, Ill., National Council of Teachers of English, 1963.

Britton, James et al, *The Development of Writing Abilities,* London, MacMillan, 1975.

Chew, Charles and Sheila Schlawin, editors, *New York State Preliminary Competency Test in Writing Manual for Administrators and Teachers.* 1979.

Cooper, Charles and Lee Odell, *Evaluating Writing: Describing, Measuring, Judging,* Urbana, Ill., National Council of Teachers of English, 1977.

Cooper, Charles and Lee Odell, *Research on Composing,* Urbana, Ill., National Council of Teachers of English, 1977.

English, Fenwick, "Effective Ways to Improve Public Education," *Managing Focus,* Peat, Marwick, Mitchell & Co., Nov/-Dec. 1979.

English, Fenwick, "Untieing the knots in Public Education", *Management Focus,* Peat, Marwick, Mitchell & Co., May/-

June 1979.

English, Fenwick, "Curriculum Mapping", *Educational Leadership,* April, 1980.

Farris, D. R., "On the use of Interpretive Structural Modeling to Obtain Models for Work Asessment," *Portraits of Complexity,* Battelle, 1975.

Forster, Richard H., Robert House and John Warfield, "Proposal for Development . . . Plan for University of Alabama. . .," *portraits of Complexity,* Battelle Monograph No. 9, 1975.

Franklin, Clyde W., "The Intent of Sociology," *Portraits of Complexity,* Battelle Monograph No. 9, 1975.

Graves, Donald, *Balance The Basics: Let Them Write.* New York, The Ford Foundation, 1978.

Hart, William and David Malone, "Goal Setting For A State Environmental Agency," *Portraits of Complexity,* Battelle, 1975.

Hitt, William and David Hamilton, "A Humanistic Model of Educational Management," *Portraits of Complexity,* Battelle, 1975.

Kingston, Cecelia, *Writing: To Assign is Not to Teach,* Presented at annual conference, Albany, May, 1979.

Malone, David W., "An Introduction to the Application of Interpretive Structural Modeling,"

Malone, David W., "Applications of Intrerpretive Structural Modeling," *Portraits of Complexity,* Battelle, 1975.

Mayhew, Ray W., "A Systematic Approach in Management: Application of Objective Tree Structure to Staff Development Planning," *Portraits of Complexity,* Battelle, 1975.

Petrosky, Anthony R., "Grammar Instruction: What We Know," *English Journal* LXCVI No. 9, Dec. 1977.

Simon, Herbert A., "How Big Is A Chunk?" *Science,* Vol. 183, No. 4124, Feb. 8, 1974.

Squire, James R., "The Collision of the Basics Movement With Current Research in Writing and Language," paper presented at conference on "The English Curriculum Under Fire," University of Chicago, June 22, 1978.

Tate, Gary et al, "Standards For Basic Skills Writing Program," National Council of Teachers of English, Urbana, 19799.

Waller, Robert J., "An Applicatoin of Interpretative Structural Modeling to Priority Setting in Urban Systems Management," *Portraits of Complexity*, Battelle, 1975.

Warfield, John N., *An Assault on Complexity*, Battelle Monograph No. 3, Battelle, 1973.

Warfield, John N., *Structuring Complex Systems*, Battelle Monograph No. 4, Battelle, 1974.

DESIGNING A K-12 WRITING PROGRAM ONE DISTRICT'S RESPONSE TO THE TWO REVOLUTIONS IN ENGLISH

John Andola
Liverpool Central School District

THE BEGINNING: INSERVICE AND SUPERVISION

The greatest single error made by every educator is making false assumptions about the understanding other people have regarding his or her area of expertise. Teachers assume students understand the jargon they use, and they also assume students comprehend the incomplete directions they often give. Administrators assume teachers agree with their educational philosophies and they assume teachers know about the theories and goals underlying the objectives of a new program. One cannot make these assumptions. One cannot even assume any two educators have the same definition for a common educational term. If you do not believe this is a serious barrier to educational progress, ask the members of an English department to agree on a definition of writing or of literature or of team teaching or of anything else. If agreement among colleagues cannot be reached on the definition of the jargon used on a daily basis, how much more difficult will it be to achieve agreement on questions like "How should writing be taught?"

The answer to the question about how writing should be taught, is a legitimate concern of supervision, since the answer has a direct bearing on teacher effectiveness. Supervision is much more than merely visiting a classroom and critiquing a lesson; it begins with assisting the teacher in formulating the philosophies which support that lesson. Supervision and inservice are inseparable, and therein lies the key to program development. No teacher can readily accept or effectively implement a new program based on philosophies with which he or she does not agree or on concepts which he or she does not understand. New programs, therefore, must begin with thorough and detailed teacher inservice, and new writing programs are no exception. Regarding teacher inservice (or supervision, if you like) the rule every educator must follow is: start at the beginning and tell all there is to tell. Everything must be stated, explained, answered, examined, and restated. The greatest asset to program development and implementation is a well-informed faculty. While this is not a task easily or quickly accomplished, it can be achieved with some careful planning. It will not be easy; it will not happen in one day, but it is the keystone to the school-wide commitment.

After a writing program has received general administrative and teacher support, and after the program has been given some specific definition by the curriculum designers, every detail of the program then needs to be clarified for teachers. Furthermore, if the program is based on recent research that contradicts current practice, teachers will first need to be exposed to those research findings and to be given an opportunity to accept them gradually before being expected to translate them into practice. Inservice, then, is not something that is planned for one conference day or for a series of three department meetings. Inservice is the continuous process of keeping educators informed about current, relevant research in their field and also about the district's long range plans for program development. Teachers as well as administrators must be given ample opportunities to attend state and local academic conferences and to exchange ideas with educators who work in other geographic areas and under different circumstances. In spite of the vast differences that are noted at such meetings, teachers are always amazed at the problems they have in common with one another. These common problems form the basis of meaningful exchange, since common problems have common solutions. Once the teacher is aware of current educational research, theory and practices, he or she can participate more effectively in his or her own district, department, and classroom. The new program based on current research, then, will by more readily accepted, perhaps even positively molded, by the well-informed teacher.

After a review of current professional thinking, several fundamental questions need to be examined thoroughly, perhaps first by the curriculum designers and a small group of teachers, but eventually by the entire English faculty. Some of the questions which need to be answered are:

> What are we currently teaching? Why? How?
> From where does direction for the current program emanate?
> What are some difficulties with the current program?
> How do State tests relate to program?
> What has been the State's direction? How has it changed?
> What does the professional literature say about writing instruction?
> Is our program consistent with current research?
> Is our program consistent with State direction?
> What are the specific needs of our students?
> What are the priorities of the community? The central office? The department?

Considerable time must be given to a detailed examination of these and similar questions prior to launching the development of new writing program. It may be tempting simply to adopt a program that is working in some other district, but this can be a serious mistake. New programs must grow from the combined efforts, understandings, and needs of the population they will serve. A great deal is achieved by engaging in a thorough program development process; teachers gain more detailed knowledge about the current status of writing instruction in addition to obtaining a clearer understanding about their present classroom practices; administrators begin to understand teacher concerns and they gradually buy into the concepts leading to the development of a new program. Inservice, then, should be the first consideration in developing a new writing program.

II
AN ADMINISTRATIVE DESIGN

Without support from the central office, even the most worthwhile curriculum program will be doomed to failure. Support from the central office exerts pressure on middle administrators who in turn foster implementation of the program among teachers.

There are several level of central office support ranging from "OK, I guess you can do it" to "That's a great idea; how much money do you need?" The central office may even recognize the need to create an administrative strucure to help deal with the creation of a new program. Such a structure, for example, a series of committees, each with clearly defined goals and an operation timeline, can be very helpful indeed. This administrative structure created by the central office will lead to periodic committee reports and ultimately to a presentation before the Board of Education, a boon for the curriculum designer. When a Board of Education supports the development of new program, the central office will increase its support and the entire process from research and design to implementation will be expedited.

Given the large size and relative complexity of organization of the Liverpool School District, it is understandable that the central office deemed it necessary to provide an administrative structure for building a K-12 writing program.

Liverpool's Program Planning Process involves fourteen steps which are basically sequential, although in practice some overlapping does exist. The first three steps comprise the district level needs assessment components:

1. Identify program needs
2. Select programs for analysis
3. Advise Board of Education

Program needs are identified by the results of a community questionnaire, as well as by concerns of the district's administrators and teachers. Recognizing that the district cannot work effectively on more than about ten goals each year, the list of program needs is then restricted and refined at a full day administrative workshop. Some programs, because of a special need such as a State mandate, are selected by the central office for a more detailed analysis. The Board of Education is then informed of all program needs for the coming year, completing the third step of the Program Planning Process.

The next component of the process begins with the establishment of Analysis/Planning Teams and ends with a detailed program plan:
    4. Establish Analysis/Planning Teams
    5. Train Analysis/Planning Teams
    6. Review Existing Program Data
    7. Review/Revise Program Objectives
    8. Review/Revise Program Plan

Analysis/Planning Teams are composed of from three to five administrators and teachers involved with the program being analyzed. For the analysis of Liverpool's K-12 writing program, two analysis/planning teams were created: one for elementary, one for secondary. After inservice for team members on their function, the teams met separately with the chairperson (an elementary principal and the 6-12 Language Arts Supervisor) articulating the efforts of each team to ensure agreement and consistency in the final plan. Committees composed of teachers are directly involved in steps six through eight above as each analysis/planning team reviews the existing program and works toward a revised program plan. The plan is then ready for the approval component of the process:
    9. Approve Revised Program Plan
    10. Submit Budget Requests
    11. Recommend Plan to Board

The Analysis/Planning Team presents its revised program plan to the Management Team. Members of the Management Team include central office people and administrators representing the various other segments of the district. After the Management Team has approved the revised program plan, the Administrative Council (all district administrators), is informed, and the chairman of the Analysis/Planning Team presents his or her revised program plan to the Board of Education. Since the Superintendent and the Assistant Superintendent for Instruction are key members of the Management Team, the plan goes to the Board of Education with their approval and recommendation, which, it is hoped, will ensure its final approval by the Board.

The last component of the Program Planning Process involves:

12. Budget Approval
13. Program Implementation
14. Program Evaluation

No program, therefore, undergoes a major revision without the participation of all appropriate teachers and administrators. Everyone is kept fully informed and many individuals are directly involved in the decision-making processs. The particular process designed and used at Liverpool may be unnecessarily complex for a small district, but whatever the district's size, if each of the steps included in Liverpool's process are accommodated, the implementation of a new writing program will be less traumatic and more effective for all concerned.

III
CREW

Satisfying the subject supervisor's penchant for designating all language arts programs with acronyms, Competency Regents Education in Writing (CREW) was launched. It should be carefully noted, however, that new programs seldom if ever are created in a void; most new programs form around elements of existing programs. Thus, the process through which a program is developed may not have a clear beginning. Elements of existing programs may meld with other concepts and ideas, gradually forming the new program. CREW came into being through that gradual melding process. It is important that faculty, especially, understand how new programs evolve so as to discourage belief that with each new program comes the total elimination of an existing program and the trauma of abrupt change.

Once CREW began to take shape in the minds of the curriculum designers, ten program objectives were identified:

    1. To prepare students to meet the State level of competency in writing as identified by the new Competency Testing Program.

    2. To comply with the State mandate that all students not scoring at acceptable levels of competency on the PCT receive remedial instruction.

    3. To meet the needs of all secondary students through an individualized writing program.

    4. To be consistent with the district's three-track system and to eliminate fragmentation.

    5. To avoid stigmatizing PCT failures.

    6. To restructure the writing strand in the current curriculum rather than merely to add a remedial element to it.

    7. To emphasize the forms of discourse tested by the State, but also to develop competency in other forms of writing.

    8. To develop in teachers, as well as in students, an awareness of writing as process.

    9. To allow students to develop writing skills not only at the competency level but also at higher levels of capability.

    10. To involve all content area teachers in the development of student writing skills.

To have all students meet the State's identified level of competency in writing, of course, must be a primary objective of the program. Achievement of this primary objective is related very closely to the State mandate that students who fall below the reference point of 50 percent on the Preliminary Competency Test be given intensified remedial instruction in addition to the instruction they receive in their regular English classes. Objectives 1 and 2, along with objective 7, which speaks to the types of written discourse to be taught, comply with State direction and State mandate. The third objective distinguishes this program from others by making it clear that CREW is not simply a remedial program. Although CREW contains very definite remedial components, it also encompasses elements that help students at all levels of capability. Objective 9 is actually a restatement of objective 5 and is included to emphasize the point that the various elements of the program speak to the needs of *all* students. New programs must be designed in a way that makes them compatible with those structures already in place. Objectives 4 and 6 relate to these concepts. Liverpool has for many years operated with a three-level tracking system, and any new program which cannot work within that system would face serious implementation problems. Objective 5 is simply a reminder that the total "pull-out" appproach to remediation often does more harm than good. Emphasizing the teaching of writing as process and diminishing the importance of mechanics is the focus of objective 8. In addition, objective 8 recognizes the importance of teacher inservice. The last objective of the program adds the element of content area instruction which has been so very successful in the area of reading and which is easily adapted to writing as well.

To create a writing program which would achieve these ten objectives, several approaches were explored, and it was decided that an eclectic approach would meet Liverpool's needs more effectively than any one of the popular approaches currently espoused. CREW, therefore, is a multi-component program, loosely aggregated, to serve the needs of the total student body. Two basic advantages of this eclectic program are its flexibility and its adaptabilty. Any one component of the program may be completely revised without having a direct effect on the other components. New components may be added to meet changing needs and exiting components may likewise be eliminated. Futhermore, success or failure of the program does not rest with any one particular approach to writing instruction; instead, the best methods and techniques for several approaches can be incorporated into the program.

CREW is presently comprised of five basic components, most of which are currently in operation at Liverpool in grades nine through twelve. Since the State's new Competency Testing Program begins essentially at grade nine, it was the logical grade in which to establish a writing program. Test Requirements for graduation naturally extended the program into grades eleven and twelve. Now, as the State's testing program moves into grade five and grade three, CREW is also, with appropriate modification, being expanded into the middle and elementary schools. Some elements of CREW already begin in grade six; others are being planned. The extension of the program is just now beginning with providing inservice for elementary administrators.

The five basic components which currently make up the CREW program are:
1. English Classroom Instruction
2. Writing Laboratory
3. The Writing Block
4. RCT Focus
5. Content Area Writing

The key elements of the English Classroom Intruction are threefold: individualization, diagnosis, and precription. Starting in grade six, a writing folder containing an individual Diagnostic Writing Log records the student's major writing deficiencies, the assignments prescribed to service those deficiencies, as well as the student's progress. Each year these folders are passed on to successive teachers through grade twelve. English teachers are encouraged to focus their class time on individual student conferences and small group instruction. In this way each student receives the kind of instruction he or she requires and each student can work at a reasonable pace for his or her ability.

Prescription activities used by the classroom teacher are called Study-Teaching Packets. Each STP focuses on one writing problem and contains prewriting activities as well as a culminating writing assignment. An STP on organization, for example, may begin by asking students to organize a number of objects into several different categories. Next, the student may be required to organize a list of words into groups which reflect similar characteristics. A third activity may be to organize a list of sentences in the same topic into some kind of logical order. After these prewriting activities have been completed, the student will be asked to write a report which first requires him or her to organize some given information. Finally, the teacher and student will evaluate the report basing the evaluation on the skills practiced in the prewriting activities.

For the past two summers, English teachers have met for two weeks to construct STP's for use in grades six through twelve. These STP's are intended to assist the classroom teacher by providing prescriptions which can also be used as models for additional activities created by the teacher. The first summer workshop was funded completely by the district; the second was a BOCES cooperative workshop.

Individualization, diagnosis, and precription are not restricted to classroom use. Those students who receive a score below 65 percent on the PCT are scheduled for the Writing Laboratory, the second component of CREW, even though the State reference point for intense remedial instruction if 50 percent. At Liverpool the PCT is administered to eighth graders in May and scored by ninth grade teachers in a summer workshop. This system allows ninth grade teachers to begin writing instruction early in the fall. It also puts grading of the PCT's, along with subsequent diagnosis and prescription, in the hands of the teachers who are responsible for instructing these students. By paying teachers to grade PCT's during the summer, the district emphasizes the importance of the test, and teachers are not forced to squeeze this scoring task into their many other responsibilities during the academic year.

The Writing Laboratory is staffed with five English teachers whose regular assignments include one period each of laboratory instruction. The laboratory, therefore, operates for five periods every day. Each laboratory teacher has twenty students assigned to him for the year. The diagnosis of each student's writing deficiencies is coordinated with the diagnosis done by the classroom teacher. The laboratory teacher interviews each of the twenty students and begins to develop a prescriptive plan. It is important that this plan be consistent with the writing instruction the student receives from the English classroom teacher. After introducing his or her students to the Writing Laboratory procedures and objectives, the laboratory teacher designs a schedule which permits meeting students individually and in small groups for varying periods of time. The instructional time in the **laboratory devoted to each student is determined by the laboratory teacher.** Some students may receive laboratory instruction twice a week for five weeks, others once a week for ten weeks, and still others once a day for two weeks. When the established goals for each student have been attained, and when the laboratory teacher and the classroom teacher are in agreement, the student may be dropped from laboratory instruction. An identified student is assigned to the Writing Laboratory for a particular period as a part of a regular schedule. When the student is not attending the Writing Laboratory, he or she is assigned to a study hall. The student, therefore, is available for instruction when the laboratory teacher is available, and the student earns study hall time when his or her writing goals have been attained. In this manner the negative aspects of a "pull-out" program are minimized.

The third component of CREW is The Writing Block. In each grade, during the fall and spring semesters, a block of time from one to five weeks is set aside for a cooperative, large group writing project. In grade nine, for example, five weeks of the fall semester are devoted to teaching persuasive discourse. Three or more classes are brought together for lectures, small groups, and individual writing activities according to a carefully thought out schedule.

All students and teachers meet together throughout the five-week Writing Block. Preparation and delivery of the five lectures are shared by the cooperating teachers. When possible, the subject supervisor and a teacher assistant are available to assist with individual student conferences. Before the Writing Block begins, students are given a long term book report assignment so they may be reading the book for homework and in class while waiting for a teacher conference. No writing homework is assigned during the Writing Block; all writing is done in class where it can be supervised and where students can confer with a teacher whenever the need arises.

The prewriting activities in the Writing Block are designed to reinforce the focus of each of the five lectures. Similarly, the writing assignments focus on the writing objectives taught by the preceding lectures, activities, peer evaluations, and teacher conferences. The final essay, based on the book the student has just read, is designed to reflect all the skills the student has mastered during the five week Writing Block. The essay is evaluated on the mastery of the elements of writing taught during the five week Writing Block. Students also receive a grade on their total performance during the five week period.

There are at least five very specific advantages to be gained from the Writing Block. Instruction is not fragmented. In the traditional fashion of classroom instruction, the teacher weaves the various strands of language arts into a weekly instructional pattern, perhaps literature for three days, writing for two days, spelling and vocabulary for one day. The student has difficulty understanding the relationship between one writing assignment and another. The Writing Block **eliminates** this fragmentation, and the student begins to trace his or her own progress in writing in a meaningful manner. A second advantage is that individual teacher strengths are put to good use through sharing responsibilities for lecture presentations. In addition, teachers can do more thorough preparation, since not every teacher is responsible for presenting every topic. Ensuring teacher use of proven but relatively new methods and techniques is a third advantage. Teachers are often reluctant to try new approaches, but given some assistance, in designing and implementing those approaches, they can more easily be encouraged to use them again on their own. A valuable by-product of the Writing Block, then, is teacher inservice. A fourth advantage of the Writing Block is that teachers are presented with useful instructional models to follow when they return to their own classrooms. Finally, the Writing Block simply emphasizes the value of good writing by highlighting writing instruction for students, teachers, and administrators. The community can also receive the benefit of this new emphasis by reporting the new program in a local newspaper.

A fourth component of CREW is referred to as the RCT Focus. The RCT Focus is simply a twenty-week Regents Competency Test in Writing. The course focuses intensively on those specific writing skills necessary to pass the RCT. Yes, this is teaching for the test, and for this there are no apologies. When there are tests that must be passed, all teaching is for the test as well as for the student. If the skills tested are deemed valuable enough to have, then they must be valuable enough to teach.

Currently, the fifth and final component of CREW is Content Area Writing. Teachers in all content areas must reinforce the kind of writing instruction that takes place in the English classroom and in the Writing Laboratory if the job of teaching youngsters to write is to be accomplished. That is not to say that every teacher must be a teacher of writing; that kind of mistake sets reading instruction back several years. No one expects the content area teacher to diagnose student writing problems and design prescription to solve those problems; that is the job of the English teacher. What the content area teacher can do is to require students to write and then structure that writing in a manner which clarifies the task, stipulates in audience, and defines the purpose. In addition, the content area teacher should expect the student to utilize the same writing skills in the content area class that are required in the English class. If good writing is truly valuable, then all teachers must value good writing; only then will students fully understand the need to write well. Science and math teachers can rely less on the objective test and require students to write more essays. If the student, for example, can explain in an essay how he arrived at a particular answer to a math problem, the math teacher can more effectively assess that youngster's needs and teach more effectively. If the social studies teacher requires that the student's response to an essay question be well structured and coherent, the teacher's scoring job is more palatable and the student's writing skills are reinforced. To convince content area teachers that these and similar techniques are helpful to them as well as to students is no easy task, but once some key teachers are convinced, the program will make speedy progress. As with any new program, administrative support must be the first priority. Then, teachers must be given inservice training and detailed assistance in structuring lessons, activities, and tests which reinforce good writing skills while also reaching content area information. The responsibilities of the writing laboratory teacher, given appropriate time in his or her assignment, can be extended to include regularly scheduled meetings with content area teachers to reinforce their inservice and to include regularly scheduled meetings with content area teachers to reinforce their inservice and to continue to assist them with the production and evaluation of instructional materials and techniques. The social studies program at grade nine easily lends itself to such cooperative projects and is a good place to begin a content area writing program.

Because CREW was initiated in grade nine, progress of the program has been greater in the high school and examples in this paper focused on that level. Most components of CREW, however, are easily adapted to the middle school and to elementary school. Structures and time periods, of course, need to be adjusted so they are compatible with existing structures at different grade levels and consistent with learning theory for younger students. The diagnostic-prescriptive approach, along with individual writing folders and prescription activities, can be implemented at any level. The writing laboratory for remediation of students seriously deficient in basic writing skills can also be easily adapted for the elementary grades. The Writing Block as a concept will work at lower levels as long as the length of time is shortened and the lecture approach is modified. Second graders, for example, might work for one day on activities culminating in writing a thank you note to be sent to a recent visitor to the class. For the elementary level, the RCT Focus component of CREW may be completely structured to deal with a very few students who in some way appear to be handicapped or nearly handicapped in their ability to write. Of course, the content area writing techniques used at the high school are almost directly applicable to the instruction of middle school and elementary level students.

Again, it must be remembered that administrative support and teacher inservice are key to the success of any new program, and those factors can only grow from a solid base of knowledge about the concepts underlying the program. It is the responsibility of the curriculum designer to gather that knowledge and apply it to every stage of the program development process.

IV
SOME CONCLUSIONS

Minimum competency tests in basic skill areas have been implemented as graduation requirements in more than a dozen states and they are at various stages of planning in several more states. No longer can curriculum planners effectively debate the need for such tests to exist. The tests will continue to spread despite the impassioned pleas and thinly veiled threats from certain unenlightened educators. The public has spoken, political leaders have reacted, legislatures have decreed. Now, it is the duty and the responsibility of curriculum planners to respond by providing improved, more effective writing instruction. The public clamor that Johnny can't write, as accurate or as inaccurate as that cry may be, **clearly places writing skills at the focal point of competency testing and, therefore, at the focal point of instructional improvement. Ways must be devised to highlight the instruction of writing and to teach writing** more effectively than it has been taught in the past.

Competency testing provided one revolution in English; the second revolution has developed over the past several years as research in the teaching of writing has intensified. Traditional approaches to writing instruction have been seriously questioned, if not completely discredited. Teachers and students alike must take a fresh look at the writing process, evaluate past experience in light of current research, and institute sound, new practices. The **Language** Arts Department at the Liverpool School District has, since the fall of 1977, been assessing its writing program and implementing a variety of changes based on new State directions as well as on research findings reported in the professional literature. The process has been a long one of gradual transition, and it continues with little sign of diminishing. Many of the ideas and practices discussed here have been operational for a considerable time, others are currently being implemented, some are still in the developmental stages, and still others may be nothing more than wishful thinking.

A few general considerations are necessary at the beginning of any curriculum project. Having long ago established a philosophy toward writing instruction which underscores its importance in the curriculum, Liverpool was able to move quickly into the next stage of the project. Since the controlling purpose of writing, it was decided, is to have an effect on the reader, this simple but guiding definition formed the basis of a developing program. Each program should begin with a statement of underlying philosophy and a basic definiton which can serve to guide it. The philosophy should not be clouded with jargon or high sounding ideals, voted upon by the Board of Education, never to be seen again. It simply needs to answer the questions: What do we want students to know? Why?

Many people should be involved in the development

of the new program. This does not mean, however, that large numbers of administrator as teachers should actually design the program. The quality of any program, experience shows, is indirectly proportionate to the size of the committee which designed it. One or two people knowledgeable about the district needs, State direction, current research, and educational practice can draw up the skeletal design for the program, which can then gradually be fleshed out as groups of teachers and administrators respond to it. In this way everyone affected by the program can be involved at an early stage, but the actual writing of the program will be guided by the curriculum experts.

Once the commitment for a new program is made, some administrators may be anxious for a document to be produced. Such a document, they believe, gives credence to the program, and, to some degree, it does. It cannot, however, guarantee teacher acceptance of the program, and without that the program will exist on paper only. To lend credibility to a new program, give it a name at a very early stage of its development. The name will slowly grow in meaning as the program grows in definition and detail. Then, when it is ready for implementation, the program will already have some degree of recognition among teachers.

In order to ensure classroom implementation of the program, teachers must be consulted at every stage of its development, and their advice must be carefully weighted. The more meaningful goal of any curriculum project must focus on those objectives which grow out of the underlying philosophy and definition of the program. If those objectives, objectives which both administrators and teachers can support, are served by the various elements of the program's design, implementation will be more easily accomplished. The document, perhaps a curriculum guide, when it is produced, has little use outside the central office since the teachers will have "lived" its design and do not need to consult it on a daily basis. After an initial review of the guide, followed by adequate and necessary inservice, program objectives and teacher objectives will become one.

IN-SERVICE: A CURE FOR SICK WRITING PROGRAMS

Doris Quick
Burnt Hill-Ballston Lake Senior High School

There are enormous pressures on the schools today to do something *NOW* to cure what is perceived in some circles as a literacy crisis of epidemic proportions. The Regents Competency Testing program in New York State is predicated on the assumption that all children in the normal population of a school shall write at minimally acceptable levels. Schools can no longer accept the implicit undrestanding that a course called Creative Writing for the able student constitutes a writing program. Nationally, there is a belief fed by national magazines and by alarmists who point to the falling SAT scores (not valid indicators of writing ability, but that's a separate discussion) that Johnny can't write. The public, the State, the media, everyone insists the schools cure the writing problems and cure them immediately.

Inevitably, anyone charged with the responsibility of ministering to the composition program in the schools concludes that large doses of in-service training of the staff is a necessary medicine. Why is that the case? There are several reasons.

First of all, English teachers often have little or no background in the teaching of composition. In my own case, my undergraduate training as an English major at a respected teacher-training university inclued 24 hours in literature, but only two required courses in composition, one a Freshman Comp course, the other a higher level course which concentrated on the research paper. My Master's program include history of the language, one linguistics course, and a traditional grammar. My program is not atypical.

Secondarily, most teaching staffs today are -- how shall I say it? -- "seasoned," "mature," "experienced."

There are few shiny-bright, first year teacher faces out there. In my own schoool, the youngest English teacher has eight years experience. This may mean that few people on the staff are in touch with the new composition work that suggests that writing to a variety of audiences, for different purposes is important; that writing as a process of pre-writing drafting, re-writing be taught; that student syntactic maturity increases in predictable patterns; that immediate, positive and useful feedback can and should be given, and so on.

Thirdly, English teachers do not write. I'm not proud of it, but until I experienced the local Bay Area Writing Project in-service and became convinced of the value, I did almost no writing of my own. I did not compose with my students; I did not write for pleasure or professional journals; I did not even write very often to my college-age children. However, teachers who do write understand the writing process and help students master it. They construct thinking and planning activities before requiring drafting. They let student see them write, pause, rewrite, fumble for a word, move the end up to the beginning, throw the whole draft away and start again. Teachers who write see the tenuous connection between thinking and writing. They see thoughts down there in black and white and can ruminate on them, develop them, see the flaws, see other similar ideas, consider new relationships. Teachers who write sometimes experience the uncanny discovery of ideas they didn't know they had --an exhilarating experience. Writers think and thinkers write, and teachers who write know this.

Faced with an untrained staff and the immediacy of the writing problem, what's the language arts coordinator (or superintendent or curriculum specialist or whoever it is at whose doorstep the responsibilty for doctoring is placed) to do? Based on my twenty years of teaching experience and three years as in-service cordinator of the Captial District Writing Project, the local Bay Area site, I can think of some things he or she should *not* do.

Let's not begin by re-writing curriculm guidelines, although new curriculum may emerge from the process I will describe. Every teacher I know has curriculum guidelines sitting unopened on the shelves. This time we do not want to change the theoretical curriculum -- the one that resides on the shelves; this time we want to change the **real curriculum** -- the one that happens in the classroom.

Let's not form a committttee to put out a position paper, although a short-lived planning committee may be needed. My teaching colleagues feel they do not control their own working conditions. They are asked to do more in less time with fewer resources. This time we want teachers involved in the decision-making so that committed change in teacher behavior will occur.

Let's not hand down directives or mandates on someone's unfounded belief that a theme a week or a school-wide guide to correction symbols constitutes a valid writing program. Research tells us that merely inceasing the amount of time spent on writing will not itself bring about improvement. And correction symbols like "sp" and "awk" are almost meaningless to students. This time we want to base our teaching procedures on sound theory and research.

Let's not bring in an entertaining expert for an hour's inspirational talk to the staff at a Superintendent's Conference Day or on the opening meeting of the staff in September, although outside expertise may be needed. Once I spoke to a staff in what I hoped was a witty and entertaining way about ways to include free writing in the classroom. With horror I later discovered I had left the teachers in the audience with the mistaken impression that correctness and spelling don't ever matter in a writing program. Since it was a one-shot speaking engagement, there was not time to bring on-going, continuous help to the staff instead of an hour of entertainment.

This time let's plan good in-service, let's make it attractive to the staff, and let's evaluate its effectiveness. The language arts coordinator should appoint a commit-

tee of about eight influential and respected teachers who present a full range of grade levels. Their charge will be to:
1. identify the writing needs of the district (where does it hurt?)
2. design in-service to fill in specific gaps (what's going to cure it?)
3. describe the evaluation tools that will measure change (how do we know when it's better?)

The committee should be provided with released time, summer curriculum time and/or salary benefits, and they should report to the language arts coordinator one month after the committee's formation.

An administrator reading this may say to himself, "Well, I'll speed the process up a bit. I don't need a committee of teachers sitting around for a month. I'll just tell them what to do."

My experience warns against that. Teachers need to have control over decisions that affect their classrooms if change is to take place. I know of an instance in which a supervisor mandated that 40% of class time hereafter would be spent on writing skills. Teachers in that district read the memo, filed it, closed their doors and went on using class time the way they always had.

A sadder situation occcured in a small city school system. There a group of teachers decided they wanted in-service, but in spite of hours of planning, the teachers were unable to get an administrator in a decision-making position to say anything but "Yes, but." There was money in the district budget for in-service. The Board had declared the improvement of writing skills a top priority. Still nothing happened except the teachers, enormously frustrated, felt their expertise was not valued and their decisions were not supported. Such are the conditions of burn-out.

The point here is, of course, a plea for teachers and administrator to work together toward improving instruction. Let's follow a hypothetical committee through its tasks.

STAGE I. Where Does It Hurt?
   Armed with the simple and clear NCTE bulletin "Standards for Basic Skills Writing Programs," (March, 1979, attached), the committee should prepare a questionnaire for the entire staff including administrators, guidance counselors, and teachers of all disciplines and all grade levels. They simply change the Bulletin's prose statements into questions and ask for responses in ten days. It will look like this:
   > What evidence can you cite that current theory and research has been sought and applied in developing the writing program?
   > What evidence can you cite that writing instruction is a substantial and clearly defined part of the English language arts curriculum?

and so on.
   In a small school, the committee members can go around and talk to the staff. In any event, the committee studies, tabulates and classifies the returns. The smart-alecky answers ("*What* research and theory?") and blank spaces tell more than several paragraphs of jargonese.
   If our hypothetical school is typical, the committee will discover the following truths about how things are right now:
   1. The staff needs to get in touch with research and theory.
   2. The curriculum guide identifies writing as an aim, but does not specify what kinds of writing, in what sequence etc.
   3. Writing of reports, book reports, essays is called for in some, but not all, subjects other than English.
   4. The subject matter for writing is almost always "response to literature."
   5. Students write in only one form: essay.
   6. Stuents write only expository essays in secondary school and only "creative" writing in elementary school.
   7. No class time is devoted to the composing

process.
and so on.

It is simple to transpose these truths into needs for staff in-service. Now we know where it hurts and we can plan on ways to fix it.

1. The staff needs to get in touch with research and theory.
2. The staff needs to rewrite the curriculum guides
3. The staff needs to learn ways to include writing in other disciplines.
4. The staff needs to learn how to design a wide variety of writing tasks specifying audience, purpose, mode, voice.
5. The staff needs to learn what the writing process is.
6. The staff needs to include the steps of the writing process during class time.

and so on.

The committee is not made up of dolts, and it sees immediately that it can't do the whole job in one in-service program, and further, some problems are more immediate than others. They decide, wisely, to let the curriculum guide go for now, arguing that if the staff is well trained, the curriculum guide is a mere formality. They decide to concentrate on the language arts staff and put the other teachers on hold for now. In short, they decide on four or five hurting places they can minister to now, and move along.

STAGE TWO: What's the Cure, or Designing In-service.

Having identified, let's say, 1) getting in touch with research, 2) designing assignments, 3) learning and 4) teaching the writing process, the committee checks with the following resources to see who can help.

First, master teachers are now on the staff. This is the richest resource. Every staff has those who are good at what they do. Well, let's identify them and give them some status and money so share their expertise. Why should good teachers have to become administrators in order to achieve status?

These master teachers should be asked to show good practices, not merely to tell about them. In one such teacher demonstration I've seen on sentence combining, the teacher hands out sentence combining exercises she uses in her own eighth grade class. The teacher-learners work in groups of four to solve the sentence combining problems and then they write their results on overhead transparencies. The several solutions are shown and discussed fully just as they would be by a group of students. Next the master teacher gives background material on the research of Frank O'Hare and others that supports the idea of sentence combining and allows time for discussion and questions. Notice that the in-service group has experienced sentence combining, not merely heard that such a beast exists.

A second resource is the administrative personnel now on staff. Surely these people could try to provide easy access to a beginning collection of resources in research and theory. (A list of basic suggestions is attached.) They could buy the basic professional library under "professional collection," make the books accessible. Then, the administrative staff could be asked to allow thirty minutes of every faculty or department meeting for one staff member to report on an article or the chapter of a book, discuss its implications for teaching, and allow questions from the audience. I saw this model work very well at a State Education Department conference in Syracuse. A lot of information got out in a hurry, and lively discussion ensued.

A third resource is the validated programs like Bay Area Writing Project and the Weehawken plan. Representatives of these programs are prepared to come into a school and deliver a package that has been proved statistically to change student writing in positive ways. Schools make the best use of these package plans, however, if they do not rely on them exclusively and without careful planning. Good in-service plans have been thought out. The school personnel can point to specific topics and areas they want to package people to work with.

The local univerity may enable to provide some help. Of course, many teachers feel that teacher education has been sorely mishandled by some colleges, but teacher know when this is the case. It can't hurt to ask if there is expertise at the local academy. The committee should ask for specific help. Remember, no inspirational speakers! Like the classroom teachers, people from the university should be dissuaded from lecturing, but might be asked to help the staff understand, for example, what the various modes of discourse are.

Every school district in the state can tap into the resources of the local Board of Cooperative Educational Services (BOCES). There's a lot more help available from that source than most teachers realize. More than just a provider of vocational education, the local BOCES might be asked to provide evaluation services, for example. Again, the committee should ask for specific help: "Is there anyone on your BOCES staff who can help us design a quick and dirty evaluation of our grade 4 writing program?' or "Is there anyone on the staff who can help us investigate possible funding sources and help us write grant proposals?" Ask and you might receive.

Then, the local Resource Allocation Plan (RAP) person is probably on the same phone number as your BOCES person. Here you might find out what other districts are doing, and you might be able to piggy-back on another district's plans.

The committee should not overlook the State Education Department. There are people who work in those buildings, and people can answer questions. Again, the committee will get better answers if they phrase their questions specifically.

The committee puts together a package of various resources which can help, but they rely principally on the master teachers who teach on the staff now. They also decide the when, where, and who issues. Wisely (remember, this is a learned committee) they decide to have K-12 teacher work together, hoping for some exciting exchange of ideas. They decide on four weeks of summer in-service rather than an after-school-sandwiched-in-between-an-exhausting-day-and-dinner-hour. They know that the validated New Jersey Writing Project involved almost 100 clock hours of intensive in-service work. They know they are simply not going to get the kind of serious attention that is required in a short course. They decide they will not award in-service credit which is often meaningless to a teacher high on the salary scale and is ultimately very costly if a Board of Education cares to calculate total expense over a period of years. Instead, they decide, as did a very small district I know of, to apply for, and receive a federal grant sufficient to pay the volunteer staff a healthy stipend to participate satisfactorily in an intensive four week summer program.

 The committee is perplexed by the question of what to do with the whiners and the groaners. Should all staff be required to take in-service or shall only the stalwart volunteers be included? They decide in-service will be volunteer and they hope for a ripple effect in the second and third year as the rest of the staff sees colleagues having fun while students learn more. The committee, pragmatic as well as learned, knows you'll never convert everyone, and they hope the weakest of the weak links will simply do no harm. Is the committee cynical? Perhaps.

To sum up, then, the committee decides how to handle the four identified problems:

  1. Problem: Teachers get in touch with theory.
     Solution: Faculty meeting time given to report.
  2. Problem: Teachers learn to design variety of writing tasks.
     Solution: Master teachers on staff demonstrate lessons.
  3. Problem: Teachers learn writing process.
     Solution: Local Bay Area Writing Project

gives in-service.
4. Problem: Teachers give class time to writing process.
   Solution: Observers in classes asked to note amount of time spent in process.

A careful reader will note that the issue of how much this costs has been carefully avoided. There are, of course, so many variables: How much stipend will be given master teachers? How much will outside experts cost? How much travel time is involved? If released time is given, will substitutes have to be paid? Is there any outside source of funding available? As a rough guideline, I do know that to train a group of 30 teachers for four weeks in the summer at a school district site (a replication of the validated New Jersey Writing Project) costs a minimum of $6,000, and varies with travel involved and experience of the Project leader. The committee goes on.

STAGE III: How Do We Know It's Better? or Evaluation of Change

In spite of the fact that most teachers and most administrators are uncomfortable with any sort of formal evaluation of program, the committee decides to use a variety of informal measures of changes. For example:

1. Problem: Teachers get in touch with theory through reports and discussion at faculty and department meetings.
   Evaluation: Principals and department heads will be asked to submit to the committee a brief summary of each report: what was reported on, by whom, what was the tone of the following discussion
2. Problem: Teachers learn to design writing tasks by seeing how master teachers on the staff work.
   Evaluation: Each teacher who attends a series of these demonstrations will produce 15 assignments appropriate to her or his grade level before a stipend or in-service credit is awarded.

3. Problem: Teachers learn the writing process through a Bay Area in-service.
Evaluation: This one sort of evaluates inself as teachers become involved in writing groups. The New Jersey Writing Project requires that participants have two publishable pieces of writing by the end of the project. The point is, of course, that two pieces of writing have been brought from idea stage to some sort of final or polished stage.
4. Problem: Teachers give class time to the writing process.
Evaluation: Whoever observes in this school system will develop a way to clock amounts of time spent in the writing process in classes visited.

The issue here is that for too long in my experience, in-service education for teachers has amounted to teachers listening to lectures, putting in a certain number of clock hours while they correct their papers. Why couldn't some simple, informal measure be provided to be certain that real change takes place in teacher attitude and behavior?

Conclusion

I've had some fun with the idea of a hypothetical committee curing the writing ills of a district, but there are some serious points I'd like to leave readers with.
1. Staff training is a necessary and key ingredient in improving writing in the schools.
2. A visiting expert who breezes in and breezes out will not provide staff development. Adequate re-tooling is on-going, continuously supportive, and may involve 100 clock hours of training.
3. Staff development decisions should be made by practicing classroom teachers.
4. Many resources for in-service are available to even small and remote districts. The best in-service, however, first taps the

master teachers on the present staff and works outward from there.
5. The best in-service program identifies, works on, and measures a few problems at a time.
6. Teachers and administrators should begin to view themselves as investigators who measure the effect of what they do.

STANDARDS FOR BASIC SKILLS WRITING PROGRAMS

An effective basic skills program in writing has the following characteristics:

Teaching and Learning

1. There is evidence that knowledge of current theory and research in writing has been sought and applied in developing the writing program.
2. Writing instruction is a substantial and clearly identified part of an integrated English language arts curriculum.
3. Writing is called for in other subject matters across the curriculum.
4. The subject matter of writing has its richest source in the students' personal, social, and academic interests and experiences.
5. Students write in many forms (e.g., essays, notes, summaries, poems, letters, stories, reports, scripts, journals).
6. Students write for a variety of audiences (e.g., self, classmates, the community, the teacher) to learn that approaches vary as audiences vary.
7. Students write for a wide range of purposes (e.g., to inform, to persuade, to express the self, to explore, to clarify thinking).
8. Class time is devoted to all aspects of the writing process: generating ideas, drafting, revising, and editing.
9. All students receive instruction in both (a)

developing and expressing ideas and (b) using the conventions of edited American English
10. Control of the conventions of edited American English (supporting skills such as spelling, handwriting, punctuation, and gramatical usage) is developed primarily during the writing process and secondarily through related exercises.
11. Students receive constructive responses--from the teacher and from others--at various stages in the writing process.
12. Evaluation of individual writing growth:
    a. is based on complete pieces of writing;
    b. reflects informed judgments, first, about clarity and content and then about conventions of spelling, mechanics, and usage;
    c. includes regular responses to individual pieces of student writing as well as periodic assessment measuring growth over a period of time.

Support

13. Teachers with major responsibility for writing instruction receive continuing education reflecting current knowledge about the teaching of writing.
14. Teachers of other subjects receive information and training in ways to make use of and respond to writing in their classes.
15. Parent and community groups are informed about the writing program and about ways in which they can support it.
16. School and class schedules provide sufficient time to assure that the writing process is thoroughly pursued.
17. Teachers and students have access to and make regular use of a wide range of resources (e.g., library services, media, teaching materials, duplicating facilties, supplies for

support of the writing program.

Program evaluation

18. Evaluation of the writing program focuses on pre- and post-program sampling of complete pieces of writing, utilizing a recognized procedure (e.g., holistic rating, the Diederich scale, primary trait scoring) to arrive at reliable judgments about the quality of the program.
19. Evaluation of the program might also include assessment of a sample of student atitudes; gathering of pertinent quantitative data(e.g., frequency of student writing, time devoted to writing activites); and observational data (evidence of prewriting activites, class anthologies, writing folders, and student writing displays).

*Based upon "Standards ..." published by National Council of Teachers of English, Urbana, 1979.

References

Christensen, Francis, *Notes Toward a New Rhetoric*, New York, Harper and Row, 1967.

Cooper, Charles and Lee Odell eds. *Evaluating Writing: Describing, Measuring, Judging,* Urgana, Ill., National Council of Teachers of English, 1977.

_____, *Research on Composing*, Urbana, Ill., National Council of Teachers of English, 1977.

Elbow, Peter, *Writing Without Teachers,* New York, Oxford University Press, 1973.

Emig, Janet, *The Composing Processes of Twelfth Graders,* Urbana, Ill., National Council of Teachers of English, 1978.

Macrorie, Kenneth, *Writing to Be Read,* Rochele Park, New Jersey, Hayden, 1976.

Moffett, James, *Teaching the Universe of Discourse,* Boston, Houghton Mifflin, 1968.

O'hare, Frank, *Sentence Combining: Improving Student Writing Without Formal Grammar Instruction.* Urbana, Ill., 1973.

Shaughnessy, Mina, *Errors and Expectations.* New York Oxford University Press, 1977.

Winterowd, W. Ross, editor. *Contemporary Rhetoric: A Conceptual Background with Readings.* New York, Harcourt Brace Jovanovich, 1975.